Managed Mental Health Care

Titles of Related Interest

Dana, *Multicultural Assessment Perspectives for Professional Psychology*

Fremouw, de Perczel, and Ellis, *Suicide Risk: Assessment and Response Guidelines*

Lakin, *Coping with Ethical Dilemmas in Psychotherapy*

Layden, Newman, Freeman, and Morse, *Cognitive Therapy of the Borderline Patient*

Meyer, *The Clinician's Handbook, Third Edition*

Sanders and Dadds, *Behavioral Family Intervention*

Van Hasselt and Hersen, *Handbook of Behavior Therapy and Pharmacotherapy for Children: A Comparative Analysis*

Winett, King, and Altman, *Health Psychology and Public Health: An Integrative Approach*

Sprafkin, Gershaw, and Goldstein, *Social Skills for Mental Health: A Structured Learning Approach*

Managed Mental Health Care

A Guide for Practitioners, Employers, and Hospital Administrators

Thomas R. Giles

Associates in Managed Care

Allyn and Bacon
Boston   London   Toronto   Sydney   Tokyo   Singapore

Library of Congress Cataloging-in-Publication Data

Giles, Thomas R.
   Managed mental health care: a guide for practitioners, employers, and
hospital administrators/Thomas R. Giles
         p.   cm.
   Includes bibliographical references and index.
   ISBN 0-205-14838-7
   1. Psychiatry—Practice—United States.   2. Managed care plans
(Medical care)—United States.   I. Title
   [DNLM: 1. Managed Care Programs—organization & administration—
United States   2. Mental Health Services—organization &
administration—United States.   WM 30 G472m]
RC465. 6.G55   1993
362.2' 068—dc20
DNLM/DLC
for Library of Congress   92–49082
                                                                  CIP

Printed in the United States of America

10 9 8 7 6 5 4 3 2   97 96 95 94 93

To Marian, Jack, and Cathy,
and to my mentors, Frederick J. Todd, Ph.D.
and Joseph Wolpe, M.D.

Contents

Preface

I began this project with two coauthors, a psychiatrist in charge of an inpatient unit specializing in short-term, crisis care, and a psychologist who owns and directs a large private practice encompassing Employee Assistance Programs (EAPs) and preferred practitioner organizations (PPOs). Due to unforeseen circumstances, my coauthors were unable to proceed with the book at an early stage, leaving me with the decision of going forward alone or abandoning the project entirely. Now that the book has become a reality, I am glad I decided to proceed.

Denver, Colorado, is ranked as one of the top 10 cities in the United States in terms of managed care saturation. I have seen very large segments of the marketplace fall under managed care control, and I have observed a wide range of reactions by the provider community to this change: denial, frustration, a mad scramble for inclusion into the available networks, and a loss of income or livelihood by those who were not fortunate enough to adapt in time.

As this book points out in many ways, the introduction of managed care into a community is almost universally associated with conflict by opposing factions in the community, most notably the providers themselves. Under such conditions, it is typically the case that these opposing systems portray each other as "evil and immoral"— a position that leads either to an uncomfortable stalemate or to changes that are forced by the stronger side.

In actuality, however, there are points of truth inherent in the positions of the provider, business, hospital, and managed care communities despite the fact that they are so often at war with each other. Directive treatments, for example, are perhaps the only types of intervention that have supporting research indicating superior outcome in reference to other approaches. Managed care, albeit due to financial reasons, is thus correct in its general preference for directive care and in its insistence on the use of outcome research to guide certain parameters of treatment delivery. It is also correct in its stand against abusive lengths of inpatient stay, inflated inpatient per diems, and fraudulent claims submissions.

On the other hand, the mental health community is quite justified in its insistence that managed care use on-site utilization review procedures directed by professionals with very adequate clinical experience and background. Therapists are wise to continue monitoring managed care for potential abuses of capitation. They are also correct to question the legality and fairness of closed provider networks, to carefully examine the manner in which each managed care company both accepts and maintains its providers, and to challenge the naive idea, promoted by some managed mental health care representatives, that brief treatment is appropriate and applicable to each case and to each disorder.

I hope that mental health professionals will use this book to understand the philosophy of managed mental health care systems so that a continued—and hopefully more compatible—livelihood can result. This book was also written to enable the business community to determine whether or not there is a managed care need for mental health services and how to better evaluate and decide on the myriad options now available. I am also hoping that this book will be of some use to managed care employees themselves. Ironically, it is often the case that people working in managed care systems have little knowledge of the history, diversification, or economics behind their business. Some information in this regard will hopefully help them with what is, in general, a very difficult job.

Since writing this book, I have left the directorship of a managed care company in order to form a health care consulting firm. As such, I am most interested in the reaction of my readers both to the quality of the information in this book as well as to the managed care factors that are currently affecting them. Comments can be directed to the following address:

Thomas R. Giles, Psy. D.
President
Associates in Managed Care
10200 East Girard Avenue
Suite C–356
Denver, Colorado 80231

ACKNOWLEDGMENTS

I am indebted to Joe Strahan, Dr. Randy Cox, Mark Johnson, and Terry Wills, former executives of MCC Managed Behavioral Care Inc., for their support of my work as executive director of MCC of Colorado. I am additionally (and significantly) indebted to Mark Johnson for allowing me four hours a week—for several consecutive months—away from the office to complete this project.

Chapter 1

Managed Mental Health Care:
A New Perspective

Landmark changes in health insurance have made managed mental health care services available nationwide. The ramifications of these developments have the potential to affect virtually every aspect of the care delivery system.

The introduction of managed mental health care into a community usually causes stress among outpatient and inpatient providers. Rumors may circulate about poor services provided by the new firm. Angry letters may appear by the dozen on the desk of the director of the new Plan. The insurance commissioner may be alerted, and diverse groups of therapists may convene.

Administrators of inpatient psychiatric facilities may also feel the pinch. All the major players realize that a new game with new regulations is in town. The resulting impact, initially at least, can be difficult. The new director of the managed mental health care company, his or her superiors on the corporate level, and the therapists employed by the company may seem to present a very threatening arrangement. This can eventually settle into a community-cooperative relationship or deteriorate into a long-standing stalemate and cold war.

One should make no mistake about the advent of managed mental health care: It represents not just an evolution but a revolution in the practice of both inpatient and outpatient care. It also represents the attempt by corporations to wrest much of the control of the payment and provision of treatment services from those who have traditionally provided it (i.e., psychiatrists, psychologists, social workers, professional counselors, and inpatient facilities). Divestiture of control tends to make people angry, especially those who perceive the change as a detriment or a loss.

Managed mental health care is a potentially positive development in the field. It provides cost containment (and thus greater likelihood of continuation of insurance benefits) as well as the capacity to improve quality of care. This potential, however, is not often acknowledged by historical adversaries to managed care—namely, substance abuse and mental health treatment facilities, traditional outpatient therapists, and Employee Assistance Programs (EAPs).

Adversaries of managed mental health care serve a governing function over potential abuses from the capitated systems that managed care pioneered. This governing function, however, may generate confusion and worry among purchasers, users, and providers of managed care networks. After hearing from a disgruntled EAP director, for example, an employer may become concerned that the new system denies appropriate care for those who need it most. The insurance commissioner may become concerned upon receipt of a complaint that inpatient care was denied to, say, a conduct-disordered adolescent causing repeated difficulties with the police. Hospital administrators and attending physicians become concerned by the expectation that they will no longer have control over any particular inpatient case and that discharge might be removed from their control unexpectedly and against their best judgment.

In the face of such charges, the majority of managed mental health care employees, from outpatient therapists to vice presidents and chief executive officers, reply that they are providing a service characterized by a *higher* quality of care both to the immediate consumers of psychotherapy and to the industry as a whole. Thus it is easy to see that conflicting opinions tend to proliferate where managed mental health care is concerned. The disentanglement of these various interests, especially with regard to the purchase and utilization of managed care systems, is one of the main purposes of this book.

While attempting to understand the values and the demerits of managed care, it is crucial to realize that both advocates and detractors voice opinions that sometimes, if not usually, mix with self-interest. Although it is important to acknowledge legitimate criticism, it is also important to determine the *context* of such criticisms so that truth and bias can be properly weighed.

A conference attended by the author, "Office of the Governor: Communities for a Drug Free Colorado," illustrated this point. The author served as a panelist and discussant (Giles, 1990c). The purpose of the conference was to convene a variety of community interests—insurance company personnel, human services managers, medical and nonmedical practitioners, EAP directors, and managed mental health care representatives—in order to discuss case management from a variety of managed and nonmanaged care perspectives. The format of the convention was a presentation and discussion of two inpatient cases, one primarily mental health and the other primarily substance abuse, with input not only from the panelists but also from the general audience.

In addition to the author, the panel consisted of another head of a managed mental health care program, an EAP director, a psychiatrist with inpatient experience on both a managed and a nonmanaged care basis, the director of a firm representing inpatient facility interests for substance abuse care in Colorado, and the director of a residential facility for the treatment of disturbed adolescents and their families. It became clear during the proceedings that criticism between systems (e.g., managed mental health care versus EAP) served in part to emplace the critic on "higher moral ground" while ensuring the perpetuation of his or her company in the face of threat.

Hospital administrators fear the threat of reduced lengths of stay resulting from the advent of managed care systems. Shorter lengths of inpatient stay also affect the income of attending physicians while simultaneously increasing their work loads and the number of referrals needed to maintain their practices. EAP directors experience loss of control from the takeover by managed care of important EAP functions. Thus, in appraising various attacks on managed care, it is necessary to separate truth on the one hand from perceived threat on the other.

Although the convention in question was generally friendly, the following, fairly representative, concerns were raised in reference to managed mental health care. A director of an EAP program from the audience complained that managed mental health care rarely encouraged internal clinicians to solicit her view of cases. This, she argued, was unfortunate because, as an EAP functionary, she saw aspects of patients' behavior beyond that observed on an outpatient or inpatient basis. Most of the members of the convention, including the panelists representing managed mental health care, agreed with this point. The EAP director went on to say that such companies deny care in order to increase profit. She gave an example of a client who stated that her health insurance organization (HMO) refused to provide a therapist specializing in anxiety disorders and, thus discouraged, the client refused subsequent care.

The attending psychiatrist on the panel then stated his grievance with long-distance utilization review companies demanding discharge of patients without actually seeing them. He believed that this was an unethical practice that unduly compromised patients and their caretakers.

The representative of substance abuse facilities argued that shortened lengths of stay in detoxification/rehabilitation facilities cut off many patients from appropriate care. In his view, a minimum of three weeks of inpatient treatment was required in order to completely detoxify most patients and to remove them from their environments long enough for any hope of long-term rehabilitation to occur. He also strongly protested the utilization of long-distance review companies in the service of managed care.

The director of the adolescent facility was in general agreement with these complaints. He had in fact been unable to reach a contractual agreement with the author's company because he felt the average length of stay (10 to 12 days) was grossly inadequate to change family systems that had been dysfunctional for years.

Each of the preceding complaints was accompanied by one or more cogent examples of the apparent misuse of corporate control over mental health decisions. These case examples, along with the complaints themselves, served to identify the following common themes:

> Managed mental health care companies put dollars before patients.
>
> Employees of managed mental health care companies, perhaps without knowing it, become corporate robots blindly feeding the maw of corporate greed.
>
> The quality and quantity of inpatient care is sacrificed in like fashion to second-rate outpatient programs that rarely get the job done.
>
> The quality of outpatient care suffers from managed care reliance on generic therapists with inadequate training and specialization.
>
> Managed mental health care representatives are indifferent and hostile to provider opinions, preferring instead to make black and white decisions based on corporately derived cost containment rules.
>
> In general, managed mental health care systems continuously place in jeopardy the lives of the very patients they are mandated to serve.

Although these themes and concerns will be discussed again in later chapters, it will suffice here to caution that, in addition to pointing out sources of abuse, such opinions meet the two criteria for potential bias noted earlier: They place the complainants on the "higher moral ground" and they serve to potentiate the systems that the complainants represent.

In response to these criticisms, the author and his managed care associate made the following rejoinders (which, of course, also met the bias criteria noted earlier). The first point was that all managed mental health care companies are not alike and that one horror story, even if true, does not necessarily exemplify the operation or management of all such companies. It is becoming increasingly rare, for example, for managed care to rely solely on off-site, long-distance utilization review (discussed further in Chapter 3). Many managed mental health care firms are instead providing their own face-to-face utilization review service for inpatient admission and discharge. Additionally, such firms typically use the attending physician's opinion as the final word for discharge and, except in very extenuating circumstances, do not override the physician's request for additional inpatient care.

Even though long distance utilization review (UR) is not ideal, it is still more workable than typically described by adversaries. For example, MCC Managed Behavioral Care, Inc., sells the services of its own UR company to employers and insurance companies in need of long-distance review and case management. The UR nurses are not free to override physicians' opinions and prefer to work cooperatively with physicians to facilitate both discharge and continued care. Given the expediency of telephone contact with the attending physician every one to three days, lengths of inpatient stay typically reduce by about 50 percent (unpublished data, MCC Companies, Inc., 1988). Such data indicate that leaving attending physicians and hospitals completely unmanaged leads to significant (and often unnecessary) inflation of expenditures for inpatient care.

While recognizing the concerns of the substance abuse representative, the author and his managed care compatriot pointed out that relevant scientific literature does not substantiate such fears. In nearly all of the studies to date, results of outpatient substance abuse care either equaled or exceeded those of inpatient care (e.g., Miller & Hester, 1986; also see Chapters 6 and 7). There is also substantial literature to indicate that outpatient detoxification, if performed appropriately by a physician well versed in this area, is effective and safe for the majority of patients (Hayashida, Alterman, McClellan, O'Brien, Purtill, Volpicelli, Raphaelson, & Hall, 1989). Thus, managed health care companies can attain equal, if not better, outcome by the use of more cost-effective means. This also appears to be the case for many mental health diagnoses, including conduct disorder (see Chapter 8).

The EAP's concern was also clarified. The patient in question had been angry with the managed care assessor due to the insurance requirement that she be assessed at one of the local offices and then referred to a provider in the network. (The patient had already established a therapeutic relationship with an out-of-network provider.) The assessor diagnosed panic disorder with agoraphobia and referred the patient to an anxiety disorder specialist within a 15-minute drive from the patient's home. Although the provider was well known in the community and familiar with the outcome literature on "interceptive exposure" (e.g., Barlow & Cerny, 1988; also see Chapter 8), the patient declined this referral, insisting instead on the out-of-network provider. The inability of the assessor to honor this request led to the patient's complaint to her EAP.

Some psychotherapy patients, especially those who are already disgruntled or who suffer from Axis II (personality) disorders, are adept at "splitting" systems against each other, in this case the managed mental health care company against the EAP. Such patients are likely to succeed with this strategy unless the complaint is investigated carefully.

It was further noted that managed care systems are moving away from generic treatment services toward specialists who practice state-of-the-art techniques identified via outcome research (Cummings & Duhl, 1986; Giles, 1992). This issue is discussed further in Chapter 8.

As indicated, these rejoinders, while possibly true, place the managed care position on higher moral ground and defend its perpetuation in the face of threat. Such discussions show that the evaluation of systems is seldom simple and that a fair conclusion is not easily reached without a look at both sides. Managed mental health care systems are not always perfect, but neither are they always evil or driven by incompetence or corporate greed. There are numerous ethical and economic counterincentives to the inappropriate denial of care (Giles, 1989, 1990b, in press; Sherry, Mines, & Giles, in preparation; also see Chapter 9). Furthermore, the appropriate use of outpatient versus inpatient services serves not only to fatten the coffers of managed care but to increase treatment quality and accessibility. In the Denver area alone, there are several dozen small companies which, due to the inordinate expense of unmanaged mental health care, offer benefits with five or fewer outpatient therapy visits per annum and inpatient benefits that are either nonexistent or similarly restrained (Giles, 1991).

Reputable firms strive toward quality care in their clinical/administrative services. As such, they have several needs and vulnerabilities that, if unsatisfied, prevent them from operating at satisfactory levels of efficiency. A primary need is for interfacing provider systems willing to establish working business relationships. When interfacing systems are unable or unwilling to provide this level of cooperation, a number of conflicts and difficulties, as illustrated below, usually ensue.

CASE ILLUSTRATION

The following is a description of the manner in which one managed mental health care company began its operations. Although this story originated years ago, it makes several points still relevant to current business climates and is especially illustrative of motivational bias among certain key systems that interface with managed mental health care.

A large indemnity insurance company, directed and administrated by a physician, was headed towards bankruptcy. Financial analyses indicated that the difficulty was caused by runaway mental health expenditures. The Plan director was acquainted with a managed care specialist who felt that, given leeway, the Plan's problems could be solved. Since there was essentially nothing to lose, a contractual arrangement was made, and the specialist began a study of the Plan's mental health utilization of inpatient facilities.

Inpatient use was 185 days per 1,000 (see Chapter 5 for the calculation and interpretation of this statistic). This figure was considered high even for the time. Average length of stay per patient was 37 days for mental health and 24 days for substance abuse. Patients were identified who had been languishing in the hospital for several months at a time.

Interviews indicated that patients were being seen by attending physician's for 10 to 15 minutes per day. The invoices, however, indicated visits of 60 minutes or more per day. There were several examples of two to four visits billed for physician's fees in a single day.

With the advent of the new program, such practices came to a screeching halt. Patients had to be precertified for admission to the hospital. Once admission occurred, a review of the managed care patient's condition, usually by the specialist himself or by someone he employed, occurred every one to three days. When stabilization occurred, discharge was recommended and arranged. No more than one psychiatric visit per day was paid, and the length of psychiatric visit—in 15-minute slots—was also preauthorized. Nonmedical practitioners were employed on an outpatient basis, and independent practitioners skilled in brief treatments were given the bulk of subsequent referrals. With the implementation of these and other techniques, costs of mental health services declined dramatically. More than a decade later, the Plan is still in business and is thriving as a major insurance carrier in its region.

Although these containment techniques are somewhat common today, their institution more than 10 years ago was a radical departure from the status quo and something of a shock to the hospital and psychiatric community. Such conditions usually lead to conflict or protest, and this case presented no exception. The insurance commissioner was flooded with complaints about improper care. When the complaints were adjudicated in favor of the Plan, the organization of psychiatrists began complaining to the Plan administrator. Since the administrator was instrumental to managed mental health services in the first place (and since they were essentially saving the business), the protests were not received with great sympathy. The specialist began receiving anonymous threats on his life. There were articles in the newspaper about the conflict and several reports that patients' rights were violated and their mental health compromised. The psychiatric community also began to vilify the specialist in letters and in face-to-face confrontations.

Since the psychiatric community was well organized in this city, the psychiatrists were able to sufficiently coalesce to threaten denial of services to the Plan unless more liberal inpatient policies were again adopted. The specialist responded that he would hire his own psychiatrists, if necessary, from other cities or states and divert his rather substantial referral business to an entirely new set of providers and institutions. These and other developments led to an uneasy stalemate over several years until the new review procedures became more accepted.

Psychiatrists are not always in the wrong in conflicts with managed care nor are they always in favor of practices that inappropriately inflate costs. There are other examples (see Chapter 9) where the tables were turned. This case illustration does, however, illuminate a typical course of conflict between provider groups (medical and nonmedical) and managed mental health care. This theme is further discussed below and in Chapter 4.

SOME EXAMPLES

This section is provided to give additional indication as to the strength of the passions engendered among adversarial reviewers of managed mental health care.

The *Substance Abuse Report* (April 15, 1991) reported that "Treatment Advocates Ask the Government to Scrutinize Managed Care." Christine Lubinski, director of public policy for the National Council on Alcoholism and Drug Dependence, speaking at a March 25 hearing, stated, "Treatment providers are being prevented from implementing sound clinical decisions for patients because managed care agents are making judgments based more on the costs incurred than the benefits derived from treatment." Paul Luben, past president of this association, speaking at the same hearing, testified, "While producing short-term savings to the insurance industry and profits to managed care organizations, the long-term cost is borne by employers through lost productivity, accidents and increased insurance premiums, not to mention the cost in human suffering." Michael Ford, executive director of the National Association of Addictions Treatment Providers, stated, "It is a national scandal that employed, insured Americans—as well as the medically indigent, the homeless, and the jobless, are unable to access needed treatment for alcoholism and drug abuse problems. At the same time, the private treatment system in America is being systematically dismantled and the public system is underfunded and overloaded."

The same issue of the *Substance Abuse Report* indicated that Red Roe, a nationally recognized Employee Assistance Program expert, recently formed a consulting company that will "take on managed care, the cost-cutting function of health care." Mr. Roe was quoted as saying, "We're trying to challenge the managed care system. Managed care hasn't turned a profit, and that's because there's no care."

Psychiatric News, the newspaper of the American Psychiatric Association, reported (May 17, 1991) that the APA has established a "managed care hotline" to encourage psychiatrists to report managed care problems involving "patient access to care, clinical review criteria and standards, process and appeal procedures, and other issues. The information will allow APA to document and challenge inappropriate managed care review trends."

In this same issue, Mark Moran said, "An investigation into the practices of a managed mental health firm operating in Connecticut has yielded a 500-page report that some psychiatrists in the state are calling a 'devastating critique'—one that may lend momentum to legislation pending in the state to regulate managed care." David McMahon, M.D., president of the Connecticut Psychiatric Society, was quoted in this article as follows: "I think the report emphasizes in the strongest terms the need for utilization review legislation in every state for the purpose of curbing potential abuses on the part of managed care companies. . . . It is a clear warning that managed mental health has potential for compromising psychiatric care of patients."

Outpatient private practitioner frustrations with managed care are illustrated in the following letter by Stuart Adelman, Ph.D., published in the November, 1990, issue of the newsletter of the Colorado Psychological Association. Dr. Adelman is a colleague of the author's who kindly consented to the reprinting herein of several excerpts from his letter:

> In the name of quality assurance and cost effectiveness the managed care industry has threatened and disrupted the fundamental elements of psychological diagnosis and treatment.
>
> Managed care groups have offered a new solution to payors. For a fee, *they* will contain costs and allow the same services to be delivered for stabilized or less pay-out. *They* will determine if treatment is necessary and when enough is enough. Carried to its logical end, *they* are not treating the patient through the selected provider. And since *they* have a financial stake in saving dollars in order to justify their service, their conscious and

unconscious bias has to be toward undertreatment and underpayment. The marketplace no longer works because a new product has been introduced but marketed under an old, familiar label. It's as if you want to buy butter at the store but when you open the package you've got margarine instead. Now there's nothing wrong with an imitation *if that's what you've chosen to purchase.* There's something very wrong with an uninformed substitution. It's also clear that the imitation may not be more healthy than the real thing and that there are many instances in which the imitation is completely unsatisfactory. No scientific data is provided by the managed care industry to demonstrate the effectiveness of their methods or the satisfaction of patients.

Inpatient Review

Managed care companies offer payors the promise of lower pay-outs through careful scrutiny of clinical services, limitations on benefits offered, and negotiated discounts with groups of providers. The bulk of clinical "management" is reserved for inpatients. Providers are asked to pre-certify patients for hospitalization and risk losing all or some percentage of reimbursement if authorization is not obtained before admission. The admitting psychologist should know and concur with the criteria being used to justify hospitalization and should take no *active* part in ongoing discussions with reviewers. Given our non-medical status, it is possible that hospitals may receive partial payments or negotiated payments on "questionable" patients while we are refused reimbursement.

The more chilling effect on inpatient treatment has been on lengths of stay. Clinicians must take non-reimbursable time to discuss the progress of their patients every three to seven days and get re-authorization for treatment. Both too much or too little progress can be seen as jeopardizing continued stay and no two reviewers see things the same way. Documentation is a key element in reimbursement and there are times that the UR person at the hospital becomes the most important person on the treatment team. Additionally, since so much time is now taken up with paperwork, doesn't it suggests [sic] that less time is available for clinical work—once again patients getting less of what they really need.

The reviewer him or herself is an unknown. Reviewers may be active or retired clinicians or even clerks. There are no requirements that reviewers have certain credentials or meet certain guidelines. It is not uncommon for reviews to be conducted across the country via phone with reviewers who know nothing about our community, its standards and potential resources. Reviewers can decide that a patient is ready for discharge against the wishes of both patient and clinician and refuse payment beyond a certain date. However, a clinician who has fought hard to document and explain why a patient needs further inpatient work may be at extreme risk if he complies with a discharge solely for financial reasons. If you ask for additional review, the process can take days or weeks—all the while the uncertainty continues about whether services will be covered. The psychologist, of course, isn't supposed to let any of this "noise" affect his best clinical judgment about treatment and the patient isn't supposed to get anxious about the prospect of large financial obligations.

Outpatient Review

Outpatient management, by comparison, is less grueling. Many companies are content to let pre-defined benefit limits and capped reimbursement levels constitute their outpatient interventions. A few companies, such as CHAMPUS, allow for a predetermined number of sessions before they ask for a dissertation on your patient. Such companies use a quasi-EAP model in which the initial interview is done by a manager and referrals are made only if necessary. Unfortunately, these screening models tend to be used to weed out patients who are not "sick" enough to warrant further treatment or "too sick" to be treated because of exclusions in the patient's coverage. The referrals made in such a model are to a small, pre-selected group of providers who may have heavily discounted their fees or at least shown a willingness to work within some severe constraints. Patients often feel helpless to complain about the lack of choice in such a system, even when they are assigned to therapists who are geographically quite distant from them. The overall result is lower utilization.

Of more concern, managed care groups have allowed payors to develop contracts with *inadequate coverage levels* and then strictly enforce the cutoffs as written in policies. Some policies were written which excluded reimbursement for certain diagnoses, e.g. conduct disorder or attention deficit disorder, although patients were never made aware of these limitations in their coverage. Contracts which pay for only ten days of inpatient service or don't reimburse for common psychological problems or treatments, e.g. family therapy, place providers and institutions in impossible situations. In some cases, access to any mental health service is so difficult that patients give up and won't receive treatment or pay for all service themselves without making demands of claims to their payor. It is the rare company, e.g. COORS, that develops a partnership with you in your work and acts not to limit resources but to determine what a patient's needs really are and how best to serve them—even if that means utilizing traditionally non-benefit services.

What Can We Do?

Well, what can we do? First, although we may find present forms of managed care oppressive, we must accept that managed care as a concept is here to stay and take steps to control it. Unofficial industry estimates are that sixty percent of Coloradans with health insurance are currently under some form of managed care—that is up from twenty-five percent only two years ago. Predictions for eight percent market penetration in the near future do not seem farfetched. Part of the uncertainty regarding managed care is that as an industry it is unregulated. *No one is responsible for keeping records or even names of managed care groups.* The Insurance Commissioner in Colorado has no authority to monitor these groups or intervene on behalf of consumers when problems arise. Part of accepting managed care must be a push toward its regulation. Since difficulties with present forms of managed care exist across disciplines and also on an institutional levels [sic], alliances should be formed between CPA and other organizations or providers and facilities to lobby aggressively for legislation to establish guidelines for managed care. The issue then becomes one of consumer protection instead of guild protectionism.

The rationale for regulation is clear since the legislature has already determined that "disclosure" is a consumer issue that must be addressed: 1) Consumers have a right to know who their mental health managers are and how benefits will be dispensed under their coverage; 2) Managed care threatens protections already afforded consumers under existing legislation, e.g., confidentiality of patient-therapist relationship; 3) The insurance code calls for specific mental health benefit levels and offers no description of managed services which can restrict benefits. The only problem with the legislative approach is that it is a long term and cumbersome process which offers little short-term relief. However, it can and should be pursued even as other efforts are made.

A number of the points made in this example are well taken. It should be noted, however, that potential bias criteria were met and that managed care representatives may have different opinions on these matters. An example of the managed care perspective is presented below in a letter appearing in the *Colorado Psychological Association Bulletin*. It is reprinted by permission from Richard Onizuka, Ph.D., Subsidiary Director for a Kaiser plan in Denver, Colorado:

I have followed with interest the current feelings in the professional community regarding managed mental health care. Some of what I write here will be not agreeable to many, but I feel compelled to play devil's advocate and "shake up" the conventional wisdom. I am not in full time private practice, so obviously I do not have to struggle with many of the current managed care issues facing those in private practice (particularly PPOs), struggles which appear to be creating much fear and threat of impending doom. I, however, am in managed care, working as a mental health provider and manager for an HMO, and have grown increasingly uncomfortable and distressed with some of the issues being presented in the "managed care debate." My distress also comes from what I see from the profession, in relation to my own values and ethics as a psychologist, professionally and personally. It is with this motivation that I share some of my thoughts.

First of all, look at the national trends in health care. Health care costs have risen dramatically, with mental health costs leading the way. In the past year, while health care costs have risen 17 percent, mental health costs have increased 44 percent. More people are going uninsured, and employers are shifting cost onto subscribers in the form of higher co-payments. Psychology, along with the greater mental health community, must accept part of the blame. I don't think psychology can continue to feel immune and dissociate itself from this national dilemma. I also believe that the profession needs to critically examine its own role in this deteriorating situation. By doing so, psychology can assume a leadership role in the profession, and effect change rather than react to it. From the perspective of a psychologist in managed care, I start with two basic questions:

1. How does requiring documentation or justification of treatment effectiveness diminish quality of service? I understand that it may be an inconvenience and intrude on one's practice, but what makes us as providers of psychological services immune from questions of cost effec-

tiveness and quality of care? If you were paying for services, wouldn't you require such accountability from a medical provider, or actually from anyone else providing you a service? My cynical side wonders if psychologists simply feel they should be allowed to continue what "they've always done," and not to be bothered or hassled or questioned about their profession, and that they would prefer that someone (third parties) continue to foot the bill and not ask any questions. Although the general effectiveness of psychotherapy has been demonstrated (remember Smith, Glass & Miller?), there is also considerable debate regarding negative outcomes in therapy, and the research data is inconclusive in its support of a particular theoretical modality of treatment as more effective than others for particular disorders. Shouldn't our profession be held accountable for the effectiveness of our treatments, particularly to those paying the bills?

2. From a personal standpoint, I get irritated with suggestions, intimations, or upfront opinions that clients in managed care systems receive inadequate or insufficient mental health care. I make the assumption that current practitioners see patients in order to earn a living, and I am left to wonder how many times practitioners have made a decision about accepting or referring a client based on his or her ability to pay (through their own means, or through third parties). By doing so, aren't you making a decision regarding the cost effectiveness of accepting that client into your practice? This may sound offensive to many, but I sense a certain entitlement from many practitioners in this ongoing debate, and also some selectivity regarding accessibility of services. (If the value is that all clients should have access to services, why aren't we all working in the community health system?)

I don't believe psychologists have attempted effectively to contain costs, to provide adequate documentation and research regarding effectiveness of psychotherapies, and to regulate our own profession regarding treatment length. I can't help but believe that we've contributed to our own mess; that our own inabilities to regulate ourselves have "encouraged" third-party payers to do it for us. I wonder how much of the issue of protectionism is not for the consumer or the profession, but for the preservation of practice style and method of treatment, and possibly lifestyle. To scrutinize the insurance industry may be beneficial, but I also believe that our own profession and methods of practice and treatment should not object to similar scrutiny. I don't believe that we can continue to claim that psychotherapy is necessary, effective, and deserving of reimbursements at current and escalating hourly rates, without adequate documentation and supportive evidence. Research on clinical outcomes and differential effectiveness of treatment, quality assurance, and yes, utilization management discussions, can be beneficial for consumers, increase the credibility of the profession, and ultimately benefit all of us. To resist such change, and to interpret and perceive such "intrusions" into our practice and profession as an "onslaught" or as "threats" and disruptions, strikes me as self-serving protectionism.

The remainder of this book presents additional information on these perspectives.

Chapter 2

Managed Health Care: How and Why It Came to Be

As indicated in the preceding chapter, practitioners tend to perceive the onset of managed care as an intrusion or threat (also see Cummings, 1987). The corporatization of care seems to them to approach inexorably, wresting a large measure of control over their usual means of practice and livelihood. This perception is in turn compounded by the tarnished image of Corporate America: Ralph Nader's (1965) exposé on General Motors touched off a spate of subsequent scandals depicting corporations as greedy entities prone to the placement of dollars before human rights.

As will be discussed in later chapters, corporate executives, controlling vast sources of capital, bring a host of management techniques to bear on the entirety of the field. The physician is no longer king, nor is the psychologist, the psychiatrist, or the psychotherapist. Corporate gain in this sense may correlate directly with provider loss.

What kind of masters will these executives be? How far, if at all, can they be trusted? Will they diminish provider services until private practice becomes a thing of the past, until the value of advanced clinical degrees deflates beyond the time and effort needed to obtain them? How did all of this happen? How did it come to be?

MANAGED HEALTH CARE TO 1965

Health maintenance organizations (HMOs) have been part of health care practice for nearly a century, resulting primarily from the opening of the West by industrial development. The Western Clinic, which opened in Tacoma, Washington, in 1906, provides a good example of this initial concept. Mill owners and employees "locked in" medical services from

14

Drs. Thomas Curan and James Yokum by paying them fifty cents per member per month to provide comprehensive treatment. By relying on capitation, these physicians, similar to future HMOs, bore not only the entirety of responsibility for patient care but also its financial risk: Any overuse of medical services beyond expectations would not, in essence, be reimbursed.

Also at that time in Tacoma, a Dr. Bridge developed a chain of 20 industrial clinics in the region that relied predominantly on prepaid contracts. The popularity of this concept threatened local medical societies, comprised of fee-for-service physicians who organized themselves to oppose prepaid systems. Such societies later opposed the onset and delivery of managed health care at virtually every stage of its development (Roemer, 1985).

The Great Depression provided landmark influence over the U.S. health care delivery system and the economics underlying it. Because philanthropic donations began to diminish, hospitals were forced to rely more on patient fees in order to continue operations. Hospital use subsequently declined while perceived need for income protection from catastrophic illness increased.

Ironically, the first proposed solutions to these problems came in the form of prepaid, not indemnity, premiums. In 1929, for example, Baylor Hospital contracted with a local group of teachers to provide hospital care in exchange for prepayments. In 1927, Dr. Michael Shadid sold hospital construction shares to Elk City, Oklahoma, citizens entitling them to subsequent medical care provided by the hospital. In 1929, Drs. Donald Ross and Clifford Loos, in response to a request by employees at the Los Angeles Water and Power Departments, established a comprehensive prepaid program to provide medical coverage. Again, however, most of these new solutions were vigorously opposed by competing medical societies, comprised mainly of more traditionally oriented providers who resisted the notions of patient control, capitation, and physician salaries. Numerous lawsuits ensued (all of which, incidentally, favored prepaid physicians). Ross and Loos were expelled from the Los Angeles County Medical Society, and Shadid was threatened with suspension of his license.

In 1932, the American Medical Association (AMA) jumped into the fray by issuing a policy statement strongly in opposition to prepaid medical care. According to Mayer and Mayer (1985), this led to the widespread development of Blue Cross because the AMA perceived health insurance to be less of a threat than capitated services. Despite such proclamations, additional prepaid companies began to proliferate to some degree, most notably the Group Health Association of Washington,

D.C., the Group Health Cooperative in Seattle, and the Group Health
Mutual Insurance Company in Minneapolis.

Another landmark development in managed health care occurred
with the foundation of Kaiser-Permanente, established largely as a result
of the pioneering efforts of Sidney Garfield, M.D. Dr. Garfield began
work at a construction site in the desert near Los Angeles where an
aqueduct was being installed to supply water from the Colorado River.
In addition to the exigencies imposed by the Depression era, Dr. Garfield
faced the obstacle of insistence by the insurance company that workers
be treated in Los Angeles hospitals. Dr. Garfield dealt with this by con-
vincing the insurance company to pay him a capitation in exchange for
on-site medical services. In addition to his well-recognized business and
medical skills, Dr. Garfield was endowed with the ability to engender
and promote unusual yet practical ideas. As part of the construction site
medical service, for example, he proposed the idea of building a hospital
on "skis" that could be dragged along the desert as construction
progressed.

Henry Kaiser was associated with this Los Angeles construction
company. He also owned the insurance company that agreed to prepayment of Garfield's system. Impressed by Garfield's work and ingenuity,
he asked Garfield to set up similar programs for other major sites around
the country. This eventually led to the establishment of the Kaiser-
Permanente health care program.

In the 1940s and 1950s, HMOs continued to proliferate but only to a
moderate degree. Only about 30 prepaid group practices were in operation in the United States by 1970. Therefore, despite consistent gains on
legal battlefields and impressive support by members, prepaid groups
remained limited during the first half century of their development.
Organized medicine and other economic threats successfully curtailed
HMO development. There were numerous congressional obstacles as
well, predominantly those imposed by senators who feared that capitated systems would lead to denial of services, especially to the poor and
elderly.

Prior to 1965, the corporatization of medical care had foundered
and probably would have remained dormant had not other momentous
political and economic forces intervened. A more extensive history of
HMO development prior to 1965 can be found in Mayer and Mayer
(1985).

THE MANAGED CARE "EXPLOSION"

Managed care developed along a legislative trail beginning with the
establishment by Congress of the Medicaid and Medicare programs in

1965. These programs were designed to extend health care to the poor and the elderly. In 1965, national health costs were $38 billion (6 percent of the gross national product). Medicare program coats were reimbursed exclusively via fee-for- service practice which, as previously indicated, dominated the care-reimbursement system in the United States.

This state of affairs continued until the passage of the Health Maintenance Act in 1973. This legislation occurred primarily as a result of the efforts of one man—Dr. Paul Elwood, Executive Director of the American Rehabilitation Institute. Dr. Elwood concluded that fee-for-service systems produced "perverse incentives" that stressed tertiary prevention and that rewarded providers and institutions for the provision of inefficient, excessive, or unnecessary care.

Dr. Elwood coined the term *health maintenance organization* as a politically and medically innocuous descriptor of prepaid plans based on group medical practice. Elwood began promoting this concept to the government in 1969. It was fortuitous timing: Richard Nixon had gained office without a national health care policy despite rising concerns over Medicare and Medicaid expenditures.

Additional facilitation was provided by Nixon's appointment of Dr. John Knowles as Health, Education and Welfare Assistant Secretary for Health and Scientific Affairs. The AMA vigorously opposed this appointee, and he was eventually replaced by Dr. Roger Egburg. The fight over the appointee further delayed the Nixon administration from developing a comprehensive national health care policy. It also caused the AMA to use up many of its political chips, weakening its subsequent fight against Elwood's promotion of HMOs.

Nixon was only too happy to endorse a preplanned national health care policy. Nixon's 1971 health message made HMOs the central feature of his national health care policy, and several million dollars in redirected funds were made available to support HMO start-up projects. Despite this initial enthusiasm, HMOs continued to have their enemies in Congress, and the original Health Maintenance Act of 1973, by the time it passed, was seriously weakened by a number of limitations restricting development. It was not until 1976 and 1978 that policy amendments led to a more workable law.

Another relevant piece of legislation was the passage of the Tax Equity and Fiscal Responsibility Act (TEFRA) enabling the Health Care Financing Administration to negotiate contracts with HMOs for Medicare patients. The Department of Health and Human Services was also then authorized to provide venture capital for HMO start-ups. Medicare began its Prospective Payment System, and a number of major insurance companies (e. g., Cigna) began extensive marketing and expansion of HMO products nationwide.

Between 1982 and 1987, HMO membership increased 300 percent to more than 29 million covered lives and 650 different HMO insurance plans (Rundle, 1987). This figure does not include enrollment in HMO "hybrids" such as preferred provider organizations and point-of-service plans (see Chapter 5). A more extensive discussion of the post-1965 legislative developments influencing the current proliferation of HMOs can be found in Mayer and Mayer (1985) and in Inglehart (1985).

COST ESCALATIONS

The opening of legislative gateways to managed care was not entirely due to a prospective congressional vision. Legislation was virtually forced by an escalating fiscal crisis spiraling concomitantly with the staggering national debt. Detractors of managed care systems do not always comprehend the scope of the financial crisis that fueled and forced the health care revolution at hand. It is only within this context that the takeover of the health care industry by corporate giants can be understood.

Health care costs have increased by two to three times the national inflation rate over the past 10 years. A major subset of these expenditures, mental health care costs, has escalated an average of 30 to 40 percent per year. Chain hospital beds increased by 37 percent in the year ending July 1, 1985. In 1986—in Los Angeles alone—the cost of a hospital bed increased by 88 percent (Cummings, 1987).

The number of people in the United States seeking health care has increased more than 1,000 percent over the last thirty years. The top three U.S. automakers spent $3.5 billion in 1984 on health costs, more than most states received from tax revenues. In this same year, expenditures for health care in the United States approached $1,500 per person as opposed to $500 and $400 for Japan and England, respectively (Ludwigson & Enright, 1988)

GTE's outpatient costs for mental health increased 46 percent in 1985. Its total mental health bill increased 67 percent to $23.1 million (*Wall Street Journal*, 1986, p. 425). Chrysler Corporation's review of its health claims found that 25 percent of diagnostic and treatment procedures were inappropriate, due either to incompetence, honest mistakes, inefficiency, or "deliberate fraud." The Department of Health, Education and Welfare tagged 47,000 physicians and pharmacists for submitting fraudulent Medicare/Medicaid claims (Califano, 1986). In 1985, medical costs alone for the treatment of chemical dependency were $10.5 billion, and the total expense to society was $79 billion (Holder, 1987).

The U.S. medical bill rose 15 percent in 1980, more than in any of the 15 prior years, to $247 billion, or 9.4 percent of the gross national product. By 1982, expenditures were $355 billion, or 11 percent of the GNP (Sharfstein & Taube, 1982: Kiesler & Morton, 1988). Costs have since risen to 12 percent of the GNP, or $700 billion (Mines, 1990). For the 10 years ending in 1983, the cost of inpatient beds rose 20 percent annually, accounting for more than two-thirds of the Medicare expense alone. In 1967, the government spent $3 billion on Medicare. This amount of money would have lasted only 20 days in 1982 (English, Sharfstein, Scherl, Astrachan, & Muszynski, 1986). More than one-third of the national health expense is currently paid by the federal government (Flinn, McMahon, & Collins, 1987). Health costs are projected to escalate to 17 percent of the GNP by the year 2000 (Davies & Felder, 1990) .

At present, one-tenth of the federal budget—and one-fifth of total budget growth—is from Medicare and Medicaid (Short & Goldfarb, 1987). In 1984, U.S. corporations paid $90 billion in health insurance premiums. This represented nearly 40 percent of pretax profits, exceeding that paid to shareholders in dividends (Califano, 1986).

In 1985, there were 30 psychiatrists and psychologists per 100,000 population, 10 times greater than in 1950. The total number of licensed mental health professionals (M.D.s, Ph.D.s, M.S.W.s, and R.N.s) increased from 23,000 in 1947 to 121,000 in 1977 (Mechanic, 1980). Between 1957 and 1976, the percentage of people in the United States seeking mental health services increased by 26 percent (Kiesler & Morton, 1988). Mental illness is the third most expensive category of disorders, accounting for more than $20 billion of annual health care costs (Mechanic, 1987). Approximately one-quarter of all hospital days in the United States are accounted for by patients with psychiatric disorders as their primary diagnoses (Kiesler & Sibulkin, 1987).

According to a recent study by A. Foster Higgins and Co., Inc., the cost of mental health and substance abuse benefits increased in 1989 by nearly 50 percent among companies with more than 5,000 employees (*Business Insurance*, December 3, 1990). There was an 18 percent increase reported in the study across all employer groups, small and large. The researchers could not conclude whether this increase was due to particular environmental factors associated with large companies or, more probably, to the inability of small companies to correctly track their mental health care costs.

If costs continue to escalate at the same rate, they are projected to consume the entirety of the U.S. GNP by the year 2015 (Jane Herfkens, William Mercer, Inc., personal communication, 1991).

COST ESCALATORS

Specialists in health economics have pointed to an emphasis on ethics and human rights—characteristic of Western cultures especially—as the "culprit" in the health care crisis. For instance, health care in the United States, is considered, in principle at least, to be a "right" available to all. The application of such beliefs has expanded into the economy in a number of ways.

The U.S. health system emphasizes and provides "last dollar" (catastrophic) coverage. This is one of the most expensive forms of health insurance (Zook, Moore, & Zeckhauser, 1981). As Kiesler and Morton point out,

> The English system, on the other hand, reimburses the first dollar but not necessarily the last. The English National Health System thus provides care for initial treatment but does not provide care for expensive treatment—dialysis, for example. The choice of the United States to insure last dollar costs results in the irony that early (and extensive) detection and treatment of progressive disorders is not reimbursable for indigent citizens, but they can get very expensive care once their health has deteriorated sufficiently (1988, p. 994).

Another irony of U.S. values is reflected in the congressional mandate for services under federally insured HMO plans: The extensiveness of the mandate ensures that cost containment successes are minimized.

For example, the National Center for Health Statistics reported that one-third of the recent escalation in health expenses was a result of an increase in services provided (VandenBos, 1983). Aiken and Marks (1982) showed that the addition of services stimulates utilization.

As employers, governments, and insurance companies struggle to control costs, opposing factions struggle, often without realizing it, to increase them. For example, union negotiators, in addition to last-dollar coverage, bargain for the reduction of copays and coinsurance as well. Hospital administrators, physician groups, and representative bodies for psychotherapists lobby in the same direction. At this juncture, nearly 45 percent of the health care costs are shouldered, directly or otherwise, by state and federal governments. An additional 30 percent is covered by private insurance companies, leaving only a quarter of the cost to the patient.

The introduction of insurance itself, above and beyond the U.S. emphasis upon last-dollar coverage, accounts in part for the escalation of health care costs by interfering with perfect competition in a "pure" market. To quote Samuelson and Nordhaus (1989), "The 'Law' [of supply and demand] stipulates that. under perfect competition, the market price will move to the level at which the quantity purchasers wish to buy just equals the quantity that sellers wish to sell." The marketplace for health care differs from perfect market conditions for several reasons, not the least of which is the effect of health insurance on "moral hazard" (Robinson, 1991). According to Pauly (1968), "It has been recognized in the insurance literature that medical insurance, by lowering the marginal cost of care to the individual, may increase usage; this characteristic has been termed 'moral hazard.'" Managed care is essentially the attempt to reduce this risk.

Moral hazard is typically discussed in the insurance literature as applicable to the consumer alone. The term, however, applies to the "supply side" (providers) as well. Fee-for-service rewards providers by use. Hospitals benefit by longer lengths of stay, higher per diem charges, and ancillary (add-on) charges. Individual providers benefit by extended outpatient treatments or by procedures that are inefficient, encouraging greater use. This is consistent with the Chrysler and governmental claims studies (noted earlier) reporting numerous instances of double billing, incompetencies, inefficiencies, and fraud. Another example is the use by clinicians of long-term psychotherapies (see Chapter 8). Since the fee-for-service system was essentially supply driven (controlled by the practitioner), there were few incentives to provide controls over such practices. A final factor of interest to the phenomenon of price escalation is a greater number of providers, including institutions themselves. In health economics, an excess of supply often *increases* both price and demand. Individual and institutional providers have proven themselves to be aggressive and effective marketers of services. The American Medical Association is viewed by several leading economists as one of the most effective labor monopolies over the free market anywhere in the United States. This dampens price sensitivity to a great degree. As Kiesler and Morton (1988) wrote, "Thus, for example, it is typically the provider who sets the fee, monitored only by the judgment of provider peers that the fee is 'reasonable and customary,' that is, normative."

Robinson and Luft (1987) looked at general-hospital competition in the United States in 1982. After the implementation of numerous methodological and statistical controls (e.g., wage rates, state regulations, hospital teaching), these researchers found that hospitals with the greatest competition charged 26 percent more—for the same services—than hospitals that were relatively competition free.

Competing hospitals must put greater emphasis on marketing in order to attract the greatest possible proportion of an inelastic supply of patients. These costs are reflected in advertising, extras in the rooms, and so forth. Hospitals must also compete for physicians and physician-related charges such as clerical and administrative assistance, hospital privileges, physician benefits, and parking. Hospitals in highly competitive environments also tend to duplicate each others' services. This is especially inflationary since duplications usually include high-technology equipment—another significant variable in the cost escalation problem.

The combination of these and other factors has led to a fiscal health care crisis that very powerful forces in the United States—notably government, insurance companies, and employers—are increasingly desperate to solve. All are of the opinion that providers, left unregulated in a fee-for-service environment, will take advantage of this fiscal system until health care becomes unobtainable except for the privileged. It is not uncommon, then, for providers to be viewed by these payers as the principal culprits contributing to the health care mess.

It is in this context that providers are correct in the view that managed care is competitive to their interests. It is also correct that managed care is a powerful force that may indeed lead to the takeover of a large measure of service control. The development of such systems, and the management techniques that the new cost-containment companies utilize, are the subject of the following chapter.

Chapter 3

Cost-Containment Strategy

The previous chapter indicated that supply-driven health care systems provide little hope for cost reduction or containment. Medicare's Prospective Payment System developed from this pessimistic assumption, based in turn on the dismal failure of hospitals to contain their own costs through much of the 1960s and 1970s (Davis, Anderson, Rowland, & Steinberg, 1990). Corporations promote management strategy as the solution to this crisis, and both public and private sectors are betting heavily on this idea.

Providers did not intentionally conspire to create the current fiscal course. Unlike other countries (e.g., the United Kingdom, which operates a national health system), health care in the United States runs under no central organizational umbrella. Some 40 million Americans are uninsured (Mechanic, 1987). The remainder receive coverage through a diversity of public and private insurance plans. The corporate takeover of health care is thus intended to provide cost solutions by organizational means entailing greater centralization of control. In order to further explain the implications of this concept, this chapter will discuss the "per thousand statistic" by which managed care systems are measured and compared, mental health care allocation within an increasingly limited economic context, and the strategic direction that will be observed with corporatization.

THE "PER THOUSAND" STATISTIC

The per thousand statistic is most often discussed with regard to the evaluation of days of inpatient use. It should be noted, however, that "days" are interchangeable: The same formula can be used to compute such performance indicators as rates of referral of therapy sessions to external providers, therapy visits provided on an internal (i.e., staff clinician) basis, and admissions to inpatient facilities.

The per thousand statistic is computed by:

$$\frac{N}{E} \times 12,000$$

N equals the number of incidents (days, admits, visits) occurring in a month, and E equals the total enrollment of covered lives. Because this figure is typically quite small, it is multiplied by 1,000. Finally, in order to provide an *annualized* projection, this multiplicand is then re-multiplied by 12.

The days per thousand statistic is linear in nature (e.g., 30 days per thousand denotes twice the rate of use as 15 days per thousand). Working backwards, the performance in any particular month on an indicator of interest (N) can be obtained by multiplying the per thousand statistic by E and dividing by 12,000.

The following example illustrates an application of this statistic to the analysis of a company's mental health care costs. This company requested the author's consultation to determine whether managed care techniques would be useful in containing further escalations in expense.

CASE ILLUSTRATION

The company employed 500 people at one site. Their mental health costs had escalated more quickly than had any other category of their health care dollar—about 41 percent a year for the prior three years. They had an internal EAP who also directed Human Services. The EAP director indicated that she was not professionally trained in EAP services or in managed care. She had, however, kept a file on each person who had contacted her. Although she was not knowledgeable about managed care, she was not hostile to it, and this proved most helpful to the process of cost analysis.

In the immediately preceding year, this firm, which self-funded its own insurance, spent $142,000 on inpatient care and $39,000 on outpatient care. The EAP director had not contracted for services from any discounted-fee provider networks, and an enrollment of 500 lives had not been sufficient to induce any of the local hospitals to provide services at a discount.

Nondiscounted hospital rates in the community were $500 per day. The addition of ancillaries and attending physicians' fees raised this figure to about $700. Insurance covered 90 percent of inpatient charges ($630.00 per day).

The number of mental health hospital days (N) incurred by the employees in the prior 12 months was determined by dividing $142,000 by $630 (N = 225.4). The number of covered lives (E) was obtained by multiplying the number of employees by 2.2 (to include dependents). Thus E = 500 x 2.2, or 1,100 covered lives. N (225.4) + E (1,100) = .20491. Since this figure was already annualized (occurring over a 12-month period), it was multiplied only by 1,000 (.20491 x 1,000 = 204.91). The company was experiencing 204.9 days per thousand of mental health inpatient care.

The average inpatient use for unmanaged, indemnity-covered companies is 100 days per thousand; therefore, the company in question was experiencing exorbitant use of inpatient care. A typical managed care target would be 30 days per thousand, more than six times the efficiency of what this company obtained in an unmanaged state.

Although this finding constituted a big piece of the cost puzzle, additional questions remained. Exorbitant inpatient use generally points to supply-driven moral hazard. This is evidenced by excessive lengths of stay and/or an inappropriate number of admissions. Unfortunately, many small companies do not have access to such data. The company in question had kept no formal records; however, the EAP director remembered several of the employees who received hospital care during the previous 12 months. The EAP director obtained releases, interviewed these employees, and determined the following:

1. Of six identified enrollees, four arranged inpatient care for themselves and two arranged for dependents' care.
2. Four of the admissions were for mental health and two were for chemical dependency.
3. Both admissions for substance abuse treatment lasted 28 days.
4. Of the four mental health patients, three utilized the maximum insurance allotment of 30 days. The remaining stay was 21 days.
5. Both of the substance abuse stays were for alcohol dependence.
6. Two of the mental health admissions were for adolescents, both of whom apparently met DSM-III-R criteria for conduct disorder. The remaining two were for depressive episodes.

The average length of stay per patient from these data was 27.8 days. Broken down to substance abuse and mental health categories, the average lengths of stay were 28 and 27.75 days, respectively. In managed care systems, the average length of stay for chemical dependency treatment is 3 to 5 days. Including adolescents, the average range of stay for mental health admissions is 5 to 12 days. Many managed care firms will not authorize admission for cases of conduct disorder, preferring to have this problem treated on an outpatient basis. (There is little encouraging efficacy data on general inpatient treatment of conduct disorder.) This is also the case for the majority of cases of chemical dependency. The appropriateness or inappropriateness of the two remaining admissions for depression treatment was unable to be determined from available information. Many managed care firms will typically decline to authorize such care unless self-lethality, or some other very serious crisis, is identified.

In this example it appeared that both the average length of stay and the number of admissions were inflated. The author indicated to company representatives that a significant amount of revenue was inappropriately going to psychiatric institutions when it could better serve the company and its employees.

Since the author's subsidiary covered 50,000 lives, it had been able to negotiate all-inclusive per diems, including attending physicians' fees, of $415 per day. Using cost containment-techniques discussed later in this chapter, an inpatient target of 30 days per thousand was established. Subsequent attainment of this target resulted in an average utilization of 2.75 hospital days per month (30 x 1,100 divided by 12,000). This annualized to 33 days per year, an expected annualized expense of $13,695.

The company's outpatient coverage was unusually rich. After a deductible of $200 per covered life, the coinsurance was only 10 percent. By a rough estimate of provider mix (M.D., Ph.D., M.S.W.), obtained from the available data from the EAP, it was determined that an average outpatient visit incurred a charge to the company of $65. This came to about 600 outpatient visits per year ($39,000 divided by 65 = 600), or 545.45 outpatient visits per thousand (600 divided by 1,100 x 1,000 = 545.45). In managed care terms, this was high by 20 to 50 percent. Available research indicates that inflated outpatient costs are only rarely due to inappropriate requests for care. The inflated outpatient costs were due partly to an overreliance on psychiatrists and partly to inflated lengths of outpatient stay. The services of the EAP director were again procured. Of seven employees willing to speak to her, six had been in treatment for more than two years.

Using a somewhat different provider mix for outpatient care, combined with discounted fee-for-service, managed care quoted an average charge to the company of $50 per outpatient visit. Brief treatment reduced the average course of care to 11 sessions. In the subsequent year, 55 employees and dependents (5 percent) sought outpatient care: 55 x 11 visits = 605 visits. Thus, 605 visits x $50 per visit = $30,250 per year in outpatient charges. This represented a savings to the company that was relatively small compared to inpatient expense. Managed outpatient expense, as opposed to indemnity, often equals or exceeds that of inpatient expense. This results from attempting to drive as much care possible to outpatient clinicians.

This illustration provides a glimpse of a few of the management assessment tools used to help companies evaluate the efficiency and effectiveness of mental health care. As economies of scale grow, savings can be more dramatic.

The author evaluated the mental health care utilization of a firm employing 17,000 people in the Midwest. As with the smaller firm just discussed, mental health utilization was indicative of inappropriate use. (Inpatient days were 267 per thousand.) Outpatient lengths of stay were similarly exorbitant. With the implementation of cost-containment techniques, this firm's inpatient use decreased to 55 days per thousand within the first year. Greater numbers of employees were directed to more efficient outpatient therapists. Savings to the company in the first year were in excess of $1 million.

These savings were not accomplished easily. The company's EAP director opposed managed care with great vigor. As is common in such instances, rumors of managed care incompetence and ethical depravity began to circulate to upper management. Managed care clinicians and administrators protested these tactics and threatened to close communications with the EAP.

Many of the psychiatric hospitals in the city derived substantial revenue from this company's employees. Following the onset of managed care, the majority of employees began to be directed to one hospital due to favorable per diems and cooperative physicians. The administrator of this hospital established an acute care unit along with several innovative partial care programs. Although this arrangement worked out well, the other hospital administrators in the city were extremely upset.

This was also the case for many of the outpatient providers whose prior histories with the company's firm, derived from observation of claims experience, indicated strong proclivities for long-term care. Such providers, finding themselves unable to join the Exclusive Provider Organization established by the managed care firm, joined together and threatened suit.

For a period, the employees were also unhappy. They had grown accustomed to a blank check policy for mental health care and resented having to come to a particular set of outpatient providers. Many were unable to continue care with ongoing providers after an initial series of transition visits were utilized. The use of inpatient precertifications and utilization reviews caused similar resentments.

Having been forewarned of the possibility of this reaction, company officials were not taken completely by surprise when faced with the onslaught of community and employee protestations. For a variety of reasons, company officials decided to implement managed care abruptly, foregoing the luxury of easing the program in over two or three years. The resulting dysphoria and opprobrium resulted in executive soul searching and second guessing. This also is a natural and not uncommon phase following the onset of managed mental health care. Of all of the sources of conflict, that of the EAP director proved to be the most difficult for company officials. He was a long-standing and well-trusted employee with obvious dedication to the welfare of people employed by the firm. In this case, however, the company decided to stay with managed care, giving a strong message to this effect to all parties who opposed it. Three years after the initiation of managed care, the community of providers—and the employees—made a suitable adjustment and, in large measure, major conflicts disappeared. (The EAP director took a position with another firm.)

HEALTH CARE ALLOCATION

From an economic perspective, managed care is one means for determining the ideal allocation of increasingly limited resources to various mental health care services. In this context, the term *managed mental health care* refers to the oversight of mental health care delivery by a third party whose purpose is to limit the care to that which is deemed "medically necessary." Medical necessity is a theme underlying much of the provision of managed services. An acutely suicidal or homicidal patient would be deemed to have medical necessity for inpatient services on a locked psychiatric ward. A conduct-disordered adolescent threatening to run away from home, however, might not. In managed care environments, *medical necessity* usually refers to the directing of care toward least restrictive therapeutic treatments deemed appropriate by various measures of clinical care and, where available, acceptable standards of empirical support.

Mental health providers have historically argued for increasingly greater amounts of treatment intensity and chronicity. The opposite preference by managed care may be judged by the provider community as detrimental to quality and indicative of greed over ethics. Such allegations may escalate and become polemic or litigious. In a health care environment increasingly plagued by limited resources, however, providers who allege foul play will be required to provide evidence that more intensive or prolonged treatment indeed leads to better outcomes.

Abnormal behavior is only beginning to be understood, but available evidence does not currently support clinician preference for intensive outpatient or inpatient care. A series of studies dating back to the

1950s indicates that although psychological treatments based mostly on insight or "nondirection" are often helpful, they are not comparatively helpful in relation to placebo or nonspecific treatment controls. Great durations of such psychotherapy do not result in outcome that exceeds that of the same approach limited to brief periods of time. (For a review of this literature, see Rachman & Wilson, 1980). This "dose paradox" response is observed with particular frequency in mental health (Giles, in press), contradicting the hypothesis that if some is good, more is better.

Chapter 8 will review evidence indicating that some brief treatments yield superior outcome across a number of disorders. The dose paradox effect, as reviewed in Chapters 6 and 7, also applies to the use of brief (versus extended) hospitalizations, partial (versus full) inpatient care, and less restrictive (versus locked) therapeutic environments. Therapists and administrators striving to interface with managed care may wish to become familiar with such research. Providers and administrators disfavoring this literature are still advised to become familiar with it: Increasing familiarization may suggest an effective countermeasure against managed care insistence on brief inpatient and outpatient intervention. This insistence is in part a result of an attempt to balance the following values commonly used to assess health care plans:

1. *Access to care:* Will managed care help resolve the dilemma of the inaccessibility of care to nearly 40 million people in the United States?
2. *Quality:* Will managed care provide appropriate implementation of treatments that yield outcomes reaching acceptable empirical standards?
3. *Efficiency:* Will managed care be able to reduce or maintain costs so that benefits are not cut and access continues to enlarge to the underserved?[*]

Capitation places obvious fiscal interest on efficiency in services, but buyers also expect greater quality and access to result. Capitation shifts risk from the payer to the provider, setting a limit (or "cap") on the financial risk of the payer as well as on the amount of gross income the provider may receive. Medicare's Prospective Payment System is an example of this.

As indicated in Chapter 2, capitation has been available since the turn of the century; however, it has never before been utilized on a scale currently observed through Medicare or through the new HMOs.

---

[*]The author is indebted to John Robinson, M.D., for parts of this discussion (Robinson, 1991).

Individual providers cannot usually compete on this scale. Capitated contracts are based on small profit margins that can on bad months run in the red by many thousands of dollars. This is yet another reason why industry is coming to the fore in the health care struggle: Incorporation allows the procurement of large amounts of capital with which to gamble on health care risk.

For instance, MCC Cos. grew as a private company to $30 million in annual revenue during its first 14 years of operations. Its expansion efforts began to halt, however, when the expense and risk of further growth overextended the company's financial base. The problem was resolved when the company was purchased by Cigna, an insurance company with more than $650 million in assets. Cigna was able to use its capital to expand MCC into each of its preexisting health care sites in rapid order. This step was accompanied by a subsequent expansion of services to large employer markets and other HMOs.

Such diversification, backed by substantial amounts of capital, provides economies of scale that spur further growth: Managed mental health care products increase the marketing options of the sales force; an ever-enlarging membership base brings negotiating leverage to outpatient and inpatient provider fees; sophisticated management information systems track costs and treatment outcomes more effectively; and an increasingly specialized base of therapist-employees broadens service and treatment aspects of the company. As subsidiaries multiply, fiscal difficulties incurred in one site are more likely to be offset by positive results in another.

Cummings (1987) predicted that giant corporations will control the great majority of health care by the year 2005. As Kiesler and Morton pointed out, government and industry will place further downside pressure on health care prices because of their monopsonistic (single-buyer) control: "Inevitably, self insurance corporations have shown increasing intolerance of unjustified costs and increasing self-regulation to contain them" (1988, p. 996).

SYSTEM DEVELOPMENT

Early managed care systems tended to diverge from one another. Each attempted by trial and error to resolve complicated issues involved in the delivery of quality mental health treatments at reasonable cost. First-generation systems tended to rely on phone utilization review through long-distance services. Reviews tended to be retrospective in nature, and many diagnoses, especially those of chronic conditions, were excluded from care. Annual and lifetime insurance limits were reduced, and coinsurance amounts, copayments, and deductibles—especially for outpatient care—increased. Access to care was often difficult. Gatekeepers were utilized frequently, and certain types of provider groups began to experience more difficulty in the procurement of referrals.

Second-generation systems implemented concurrent utilization reviews for hospital stays, and utilization specialists performed their work directly on site. Criteria were developed specifying more clearly the permissible conditions under which inpatient use would be paid. Insurance companies began to subcontract with or purchase EAP and managed mental health care firms. More refined systems for gatekeepers (HMOs and PPOs) were developed, and a new emphasis on brief treatments was observed. Reimbursements favored in-plan versus out-of plan-providers, including institutions. Nonmedical practitioners were more frequently utilized.

Bonus systems paid providers and managers for improved fiscal results. Shorter lengths of stay were authorized (3 to 5 days versus 3 to 5 weeks). Some of the prior difficulties with access and diagnostic exclusions began to be resolved, due in part to the "medical cost offset" effect following psychotherapeutic intervention (see Chapter 5). Exclusion continued, however, for the "worried well": Gatekeepers were instructed to direct authorizations for outpatient care only to those truly in need.

The third generation of managed mental health care saw the development of increasing numbers of HMOs along with greater sophistication with the computation of capitation payments, performance bonuses, and outpatient benefits. As management of inpatient use became a more predominant focus, copayments for outpatient care tended to go down. Some systems paid 100 percent for the first 5 or 10 outpatient visits, increasing copays as utilization increased. Physicians were sometimes paid for an entire week's work of inpatient care regardless of whether the patient was discharged from the hospital on the first or the seventh day after admission. More aggressive case management was observed. For example, some companies sent assessors into emergency rooms to prevent hospitalization and to divert cases to less restrictive forms of care. Acute care specialists were hired to oversee treatment from start to finish, including frequent contacts with physicians to facilitate discharge from the hospital. Managed care companies developed sophisticated contracts requiring, among other things, that contractees cooperate with utilization review. Standard treatment protocols by disorder were assigned. Preferred practices were identified on 8 to 20 session models by disorder (see Chapter 8), and management information systems tracked more completely provider proficiency by diagnosis and severity.

Third-generation systems comprise what is available now. The fourth generation of managed mental health care is anyone's guess. However, it is likely that many of the previously established systems will be accompanied by a new wave of refinements. Provider tracking systems may develop more extensively, eventually including a means of tracking relapse by diagnosis by provider. Therapists may be required to account for their services with measurable outcomes. There may be increasing emphasis on valid and reliable questionnaire assessment by disorder. Much greater emphasis will probably be placed on the development of alternatives to hospitalization, especially those with emphasis on management of crisis care (see Chapter 7). There will be more sophisticated methodology for the management of chronic conditions (borderline personality disorder, treatment-reactive schizophrenia). There will be a growing use of specialists and more reliance on second opinions, especially with regard to inpatient use. Managed care companies will probably control the great majority of care, and private practice, as we know it, may be relegated more predominantly to practitioners with clients able and willing to finance treatment costs. As Mines (1990) stated, "The future is empiricism."*

---

* The author is also indebted to Robert Mines, Ph.D., of Mines and Associates for his discussions with the author on generational developments in managed mental health care (Mines, 1990).

Chapter 4
Practitioner's Guide

Managed mental health care encompasses a bewildering array of practice recommendations, patterns of inpatient and outpatient utilization, and contractual arrangements. Each company has its own distinct methods of operation on a community level and, if applicable, on a national or corporate level. When attempting to understand and evaluate any particular managed care firm, it is generally useful to obtain an idea not only about the mission of the company but also about the mission's implementation in local practice.

Mission statements and business philosophies can be found in self-descriptive information published by the company (see Chapter 10). Updates on new material should be obtained wherever possible. It is also useful to obtain data about managed care companies from external sources of review. These include the *Wall Street Journal*, *Modern Health Care*, the *Journal of Hospital and Community Psychiatry*, the *Managed Care Newsletter*, and the *Employee Assistance Monthly*. Especially useful sources of information originate from employees working at the local site. The availability of local sources varies according to whether the company's provider list is open or closed.

The closed provider list is an obstacle facing many practitioners attempting to participate in managed mental health care service delivery. Some companies employ their own therapists and do not refer to independent practitioners. This arrangement, by definition, excludes other providers from obtaining a participant status. Other types of "closed" system arrangements, however, can be joined.

CLOSED PROVIDER LISTS

Closed provider lists are a frustrating fact of life to practitioners wishing to obtain referrals from managed mental health care. It is important to

note, however, that closed provider lists are often a frustration for the
managed care firm as well. Consider, for example, the following comments from the executive director of a managed care firm whose situation was less than ideal:

> We opened our operations in this city with a contingent of only 12,000
> members, all of whom were covered by an HMO insurance vendor.
> Although some of our company's subsidiaries around the country have
> had trouble finding providers willing to participate, we had just the oppo-
> site problem.
>
> The HMO insurance company here was unhappy with its prior con-
> tractee for mental health services. This group was formed by a local inpa-
> tient mental health facility and comprised mainly of therapists who hospi-
> talized there. As an entrepreneurial business venture, the hospital decided
> to take the plunge and go fully at risk by capitating all mental health and
> substance abuse services within the HMO's catchment area. Unfortunately
> for the hospital and its provider group, their relative inexperience with
> managed care led to bidding their capitation too low, managing inpatient
> stays too loosely, and failing to establish good working relationships with
> the administrators of the HMO. As a result, their contract was not renewed,
> and our company was asked to take over.
>
> The takeover led to hard feelings toward our company, and, in an
> attempt to solve this problem, our vice president decided to make the hos-
> pital our primary inpatient facility and to extend provider applications to
> all of the members in the hospital's PPO. Although this strategy definitely
> improved the process of our integration into the community, it also caused
> me a number of difficulties that I am still dealing with more than three
> years after our operations began.
>
> In the first place, their PPO was comprised mainly of psychiatrists. Our
> firm likes working with psychiatrists, but they usually comprise only 25
> percent of our provider quotient. The hospital's PPO network consisted of
> a physician contingent of nearly 80 percent. They already had obtained a
> bad taste for managed care by the disastrous experience with the HMO,
> and, though some were very sophisticated in managing inpatient care, the
> majority either would not or could not cooperate with what we really
> wanted. The majority had been trained in long term, psychoanalytically
> oriented therapies, thereby negating much of the outpatient philosophy of
> our company. As if this were not bad enough, nearly all of the PPO
> providers joined, and we were immediately flooded with 80 or more
> providers, most of whom either were not needed or did not fit with our
> philosophy. This overload on our system prevented us from adding other
> providers who were more compatible with our approach.

This director was obviously in need of a new set of providers for
his clinic. A need had been created, and the right providers, knowing
how to proceed, would eventually have filled it. This is by no means an
uncommon scenario. With patience and tact, many closed provider systems can eventually be joined. Patience is required because the attrition

rate can be slow. Providers retire and move out of state. They become disenchanted with the managed care firm (or vice versa). The company's catchment area may expand or the need for a new or a different level of care provider may be realized, but all of these things take time. Even when the need to delete providers becomes evident, many contracts prevent this from occurring except for a window of time that occurs once in the calendar year. There is also an emotional inertia that may slow deletions (i.e., directors are often reluctant to deal with the ensuing disappointment from a provider who has been dropped from a list). (The author received an angry letter from a deleted provider even though the provider had left the state and had no plans to return.) Thus, the window of opportunity to join a closed provider list may take several seasons before it lets in fresh air, and the prior tact and skill (or lack thereof) of prospective providers will determine the composition of the new members on the list.

Avenues into a provider list may originate from several locations, as, for instance, with a casual conversation with the firm's utilization review nurse. Managed care companies are invariably looking for compatible providers, and a physician who has a friendly and responsive presence quickly becomes known. Clinicians who work for the firm will also inform the director about compatible providers to pursue.

Administrators of managed care companies are under pressure to provide high-quality services that are efficient and readily accessible. Provider lists that are officially closed are still vulnerable to the infiltrator who has a particular geographical location and/or specialization in need. It is often possible to take the director to lunch in order to discuss these options. If this is infeasible or unwelcome, the administrator will often consent to a 15-minute office appointment. This is a good strategy even if it takes several weeks or months to get on the calendar.

The director or chief administrator is not always the person who decides on the status of the provider list. There may be a clinical director, an office manager, or a clinician who has this responsibility, and the name of the designee can be obtained by placing a call to the office. This person may be more accessible than the director.

The best approach to penetrating closed provider lists is via information-gathering interviews. With this approach, the provider does not begin by attempting to "sell" his or her services and specializations but instead makes arrangements to meet one or more of the firm's employees in order to get a better idea of its philosophies, key employees, and needs. Once this information has been gathered, the provider is in a better position to increase the firm's receptiveness to the professional services that he or she is attempting to sell.

CASE ILLUSTRATION 1

A psychologist in a large city in the midwest wanted to join the provider list of a 300,000-member HMO that had established an exclusive provider network for mental health services. The word around town was that psychologists and all other nonmedical practitioners were excluded from provider status for this company, and several of the psychologist's medical associates confirmed the bad news. However, these associates also provided the psychologist with information about the Plan that was then used to form strategy.

The psychologist specialized in the outpatient treatment of adults suffering from anxiety disorders, depression, substance abuse, and eating disorders. He learned from his information interviews that the Plan ran its own substance abuse treatment program internally and that psychiatrists were used exclusively to treat anxiety disorders, depression, and general adult disturbances. He noted, however, that there were four hospitals in the city that were heavily advertising their inpatient services for the treatment of eating disorders, including bulimia nervosa.

The psychologist had been following research indicating that inpatient care for bulimia was not unusually effective and that new treatments based on exposure models (see Chapter 8) were obtaining fairly rapid treatment gains for the majority of patients. Understanding managed care interest in avoiding or reducing inpatient use, this psychologist surmised that the Plan had probably experienced unwelcome pressure from patients and physicians to provide hospitalization for bulimic individuals.

He scheduled a 20-minute appointment with the vice president of mental health for the Plan, a psychiatrist who controlled the status of the provider list. Before the meeting, the psychologist sent this vice president a brief letter stating his specialization in eating disorders and his emerging ability to treat such problems on an outpatient basis. He included a journal article delineating the methodology and the effectiveness of the new approach.

This psychologist learned through colleagues that Plan benefits included 20 lifetime visits per disorder and that all visits after 10 were approved in five-session blocks following utilization review. With this information, the psychologist was able to focus his 20 minutes directly on the eating disorder issue. He explicated his approach and referenced relevant outcome literature. He explained that the average number of visits needed to obtain significant improvement varied between 8 and 17 and offered to cooperate fully with the Plan's utilization review procedures for provision and extension of outpatient care. He gave the vice president a clear indication of willingness to work with psychiatrists and of a working knowledge of the coordination of his treatment with psychopharmacological approaches to bulimia nervosa. The vice president agreed to give the psychologist a try.

The vice president had a need, previously identified by the psychologist, to provide quality treatment for eating disorders that was considerably less expensive than hospital care. This need in turn generated a willingness to experiment with a nonmedical practitioner, and a reciprocal business relationship developed from there. The psychologist now receives a third of his income from this referral source. The Plan has begun to refer additional disorders as well.

CASE ILLUSTRATION 2

A colleague of the author's was at a party where she overheard the director of a local Kaiser plan bemoaning a lack of staff therapists trained in the treatment of certain children's disorders. The Kaiser plan typically operates on a staff model, making few external referrals to individual practitioners, and the Kaiser clinic in question was no exception. However, armed with knowledge of need, this psychologist was able to approach the director informally at the party—and formally thereafter in an interview at his office—about her ability to treat the children's disorders comprising Kaiser's coverage gap.

This clinician was also aware of the relevant outcome literature documenting the most effective means of approach to these problems. She worked hard to cooperate with Kaiser representatives, and she eventually became respected and valued by the Plan. Subsequent data on her treatment services indicated that they were as cost effective as hiring internal staff. Consequently, Kaiser kept sending her business on an external basis.

OPEN PROVIDER LISTS

Open provider lists are, by definition a type of "open season" for all comers who meet credentialing standards of the firm. Open provider lists have the disadvantage of encouraging provider surpluses, and many provider members become relegated to referral limbo where they can languish for years. The techniques most useful for avoiding this dilemma are equivalent to those mentioned earlier: *Obtain information interviews until sufficient knowledge permits a direct approach to the persons most responsible for referral control.*

Once such obstacles are overcome, the receipt of cases becomes a double-edged sword. Each and every case, despite perhaps dozens of successful treatment experiences and the establishment of a good working relationship with the Plan, becomes an opportunity either for the continuation of the relationship or for the development of problems, which can be ruinous. It takes only one difficult case for a hard-earned relationship with a managed mental health care firm to go downhill.

Managed care professionals do not expect all cases to be successful when referred for outpatient care. Some problems are going to remain unresolved, and no therapist is liked by every member of his or her clientele. The handling of problem cases or patient complaints, however, determines in large measure whether or not subsequent referrals will recur. (An example is provided in one of the case illustrations that follows.)

There is another threat to the stability of Plan-provider referral relationships. This is the phenomenon of *provider complacency* which tends to occur as increasing amounts of time and experience with the Plan accumulate. It is very easy for a provider to take the referral relationship for granted over time and to begin to resent the reporting requirements that the Plan uses to monitor and authorize outpatient or inpatient care. Provider complacency can then manifest in several ways, which Plan employees become aware of and subsequently resent. (This common threat to referral relations is also illustrated later.)

MEDICAL PRACTITIONERS

Managed mental health care tends to affect psychiatric practice to a significant extent. Managed care firms typically refer to nonmedical practitioners for outpatient care and reserve psychiatric treatment for medication management and inpatient work (Flinn, McMahon, & Collins, 1987). A number of such firms deny administrative positions to psychiatrists. The psychiatrist's work is closely monitored. Outpatient and inpatient sessions must be preauthorized, and a utilization review specialist is often involved to ensure that the psychiatrist moves cases through the hospital in an efficient fashion. These and other policies have relegated psychiatrists to positions that entail impressment of their control over clinical and administrative decisions.

Psychiatrists have been trained to view themselves as leaders in the provision and administration of mental health services. Under traditional arrangements, psychiatrists bill more money for their appointments, assume primary responsibility for the supervision of other therapists' work, and provide substantial policy input on both a local and a nationwide basis. Thus, the divestiture of control to nonmedical personnel and practitioners has been a large and sometimes bitter pill for psychiatrists to swallow when they attempt to work within the confines of managed care.

In communities where managed care is new, the most serious and bitter conflicts tend to originate from the psychiatric community.

However, some psychiatrists have blended remarkably well with these systems. (Examples of these instances are illustrated later; also see Chapter 1.)

Despite adopting practice patterns that diverge from those condoned by indemnity insurers, managed mental health care is still greatly in need of psychiatrists. Without psychiatric input, managed care firms cannot work well, if at all. The main reason for this dependence is the control that psychiatrists have over the utilization of psychotropic medications.

Psychopharmacology has greatly advanced the field, especially within the last 20 years. Neuroleptic drugs have been effective in controlling many of the positive signs of schizophrenia. Antidepressants have demonstrated a fairly consistent superiority to placebo for such disorders as unipolar depression and panic disorder. Similarly, lithium carbonate has provided a nearly miraculous palliative for many cases of manic depressive illness. Nonpsychiatric physician-practitioners are often reluctant to treat such patients. The psychiatrist is thus a crucial component of the managed mental health network.

As indicated in other chapters, the fiscal effectiveness of managed mental health care systems has resulted primarily from the reduction of inpatient lengths of stay. Although this is accompanied by the worry that stays are too short (see Chapter 9), managed care firms would never have gained such a foothold had not the prior system been taken advantage of or abused. In Chapters 6 and 7, research literature is discussed indicating that therapeutic communities long promoted extended durations of inpatient care despite lack of outcome superiority over treatments less intensive or prolonged. Psychiatrists who insist upon long inpatient stays run into conflicts with managed care.

Another complicating factor has been the emphasis on Freudian psychotherapies in medical schools and psychiatric residencies. Unfortunately, these types of intervention have been characterized by very long durations of outpatient care, discouraging results in the outcome literature, and reactance of proponents to the acquisition of newer treatment methods based on continuing research. (Nonmedical practitioners have also been guilty of this.) Freudian practices have been criticized from quite a number of perspectives, including theory construction (e.g., Holt, 1965), philosophy of science (Cioffi, 1960), and empirical outcome (e.g., Giles, 1983a; 1983b; 1992; Salter, 1963; Stuart, 1977), yet they continue to be the principal mode of indoctrination to medical school students around the country (Wolpe, 1990). Once professionals are indoctrinated in this school of thought, they very rarely change (Garfield, 1980). The preference of managed care for more short-term, goal-oriented therapies is somewhat foreign to many psychiatric (and other) practitioners and provides yet another source of friction for those whose leanings are toward a more traditional approach.

Managed care personnel fear psychiatrists who are overly controlling or domineering. Such feelings hinder attempts by managed care and psychiatry to conduct business together. It is very easy for signals to get crossed under such circumstances, and psychiatrists must display a great deal of tact to avoid such problems. In most circumstances, psychiatrists can help themselves immeasurably by giving the impression of a willingness to work cooperatively with the managed managerial system as well as with nonmedical practitioners. They are well advised to state an interest in and, where accurate, a compatibility with the utilization of brief psychotherapeutic interventions. Appropriate reference material includes Beck, Rush, Shaw, and Emery (1979), de Shazer (1985), Michelson and Ascher (1987), Wilson and O'Leary (1980), and Wolpe (1990). An impression of interpersonal ease, sense of humor, and anger control will help the participating psychiatrist stand out among his or her peers who still may be clinging to traditional roles and attempting to force them into the metal tumblers of the mindset of managed care.

It is not suggested that psychiatrists adopt a role with which they are uncomfortable just for the purpose of working with managed care. Managed care is not for everyone, and each psychiatrist should carefully evaluate personal compatibility with this approach. Some psychiatrists prefer to avoid managed care whenever possible. Managed care personnel are sensitive to this attitude and can develop it into a number of problems and miscommunications.

Due to the diversity of managed care systems, the same psychiatrist can be perfectly compatible with one company and perfectly incompatible with another. Sometimes the degree of compatibility can be determined only by experience; however, there are certain a priori clues given by managed health care as to provider friendliness. These are sometimes contained in the firm's contractual language. Guidelines to the practitioner in this regard are available at the end of this chapter.

Examples of ideal and problematic interactions with managed mental health care firms are illustrated here.

CASE ILLUSTRATION 3

A 50,000-member Plan was directed by a social worker at a local subsidiary of a large, nationally based firm. He was interrupted by a tearful secretary who asked for help fielding a call from an irate psychiatrist. The director took the call and asked about the problem. The psychiatrist, an independent contractor with the firm, voiced a complaint that the secretary had been "hassling" him because a suicidal patient of his had been in the hospital for 16 days. According to the psychiatrist, the secretary said, "Our average length of stay is only 14 days for such cases and so we were wondering when you might arrange for her discharge."

The director commiserated with the psychiatrist about this interaction but also stated that the use of obscenities with the secretary was not really necessary. The director indicated a willingness to talk with the secretary about the exchange, but he added that such difficulties could be handled in a more tactful way. He asked the psychiatrist to contact him directly in the future should the psychiatrist experience any further difficulties of this sort. He also assured the psychiatrist that lengths of stay in such circumstances were determined by the individualities of each particular case and that he would be willing to consider extending the inpatient stay further.

The psychiatrist was unmollified by this exchange. He reiterated, quite angrily, that secretaries should not be functioning in a utilization review role, and he questioned the integrity of the director and of the HMO that the director served. He stated that the Plan's medical director was "just a puppet of the corporation." The psychiatrist ended by stating that the reimbursement from the Plan was inadequate and questioned why he should accept $93 per inpatient visit when his typical fee was $140 .

The social worker replied that he was fully assured of his medical director's competence and integrity and that the psychiatrist's allegations were both inaccurate and severe. He gave the psychiatrist inpatient authorization over the telephone to extend the patient's stay up to the 30 days allowable under the insurance benefit. The director then indicated that the Plan would not be troubling the psychiatrist with any further referrals. The next morning, the director mailed a letter providing formal notice of the termination of the psychiatrist's contractual relationship as an independent provider to the Plan.

As is often the case, this exchange had other consequences down the road. The psychiatrist took a position a year later as medical director of a local inpatient facility. The facility's chief administrator, who had not looked into the psychiatrist's history with managed care plans, made a call to the Plan director in order to solicit inpatient referral business. The director replied that his experience with the administrator's hospital had been satisfactory but that referrals to this facility would not be forthcoming due to the difficulties that had ensued with the hospital's new medical director.

Although it is easy to sympathize with the psychiatrist's frustrations, his use of a different approach may well have prevented the ensuing ramifications. Had the psychiatrist negotiated with the director in a different fashion, the inpatient stay would probably have been extended, and an ongoing working relationship with the psychiatrist would have continued uninterrupted. The ensuing consequences extended not only to the psychiatrist and to the hospital he eventually directed but also throughout the local plan—that is, the Plan's administrators and clinicians began to expect such behavior from all psychiatrists, and subsequent wariness, suspiciousness, and defensiveness increased.

CASE ILLUSTRATION 4

This scenario began in the southeast with an HMO insurance plan capitating its mental health and substance abuse services to a local subsidiary of a managed mental health care firm. This insurance plan also capitated its health services to local physician groups and approached one such group, the Riverside Physician Associates, to provide general outpatient services in the southwest section of the city.

Riverside employed a variety of practitioners—specializing in family medicine, internal medicine, and so forth—as well as two psychiatrists. Since the HMO's mental health services were subsumed by the managed care provider and since the HMO was looking for health (versus mental health) subcontractors, the two Riverside psychiatrists were excluded from the membership invitation. One of the two psychiatrists concluded that she had been "blackballed" by the managed mental health care firm.

This psychiatrist neither called the managed mental health care firm to inquire about joining its provider group nor consulted with the HMO as to why she had been excluded from the invitation. Instead, she contacted the general manager of the HMO to say that the subcontractor for mental health services (i.e. the managed mental health care firm) was directed by incompetent administrators. She alleged that the executive director of the managed mental health company, Dr. Smith, had been fired under shameful circumstances from a former position. The psychiatrist stated that Dr. Smith had unfairly excluded her from the provider network because of professional jealousy. Upon further questioning, the psychiatrist stated that she had attempted to join the provider group but that Dr. Smith had been very rude to her during a phone conversion and had uttered several obscenities and threats. The psychiatrist then stated that this firm's medical director was "old and incompetent" and that either a new firm or a new medical and executive director were badly needed. The psychiatrist ended the conversation by threatening to sue if she continued to be excluded from this list.

The general manager finished this conversation feeling quite worried. Although his prior relationship with the executive and medical directors had been good, his confidence had been shaken by the psychiatrist's remarks. He worried about his responsibility in the decision to contract with this particular firm. He worried about the possibility of a substantial portion of his membership going to a clinic whose services were overseen by a medical director and an executive director who were possibly incompetent or otherwise unsavory. He also began to worry about the financial stability of the managed mental health care company, knowing from observation how quickly financial ruin can occur with such firms when they mismanage annual revenues (in this case $12 million). After thinking about this matter, he decided to directly relay what the psychiatrist said.

The news was very upsetting both to the executive director and to the medical director of the firm. Having worked very hard to establish a good relationship with the HMO and its general manager, they feared that this relationship had been destroyed by the psychiatrist's call. They did not want to be responsible to the parent corporation for the eventual loss of $12 million in annual revenues. They did not wish to lose their jobs, and they worried that subsequent complaints to the HMO might be viewed, by the general manager especially, in a different light. They decided to schedule an appointment with him to discuss the matter further.

By the time the meeting could be arranged, the vice president of operations of the parent corporation had been apprised by Dr. Smith of the psychiatrist's complaint. The vice president consulted with Dr. Smith and the medical director about how to proceed. At the meeting, Dr. Smith stated that he had not been fired from his former position. He brought along a copy of his last performance evaluation at the hospital and a written statement, obtained by the parent corporation when considering Dr. Smith as a new hire, that the hospital would be happy to employ Dr. Smith again in the future. Dr. Smith gave the HMO director the name of his former boss at the hospital and told him to feel free to call should there be any additional questions or concerns. Dr. Smith also denied using any obscenities with the complainant and in fact denied having any prior contact with her at all.

Dr. Smith presented evidence that his medical director was highly respected in the city. This served to restore favorable impressions about the managed mental health care firm. Fortunately for Dr. Smith, the psychiatrist who initially lodged the complaint had developed a reputation in the city for obstreperousness and unreasonable behavior. The HMO director became aware of this after making several inquiries into the nature of the complaint.

As with the prior case illustration, the psychiatrist in question was employed at a hospital attempting to gain more referral business from managed mental health care firms. The chief administrator of this hospital had been negotiating a facility contract with Dr. Smith. Dr. Smith called this administrator to inform him that such negotiations would need to be discontinued until the psychiatrist's complaint was resolved. Dr. Smith explained that it did not appear to him wise to refer to a hospital whose primary medical practitioner had such a negative opinion of the firm. The administrator apologized profusely, stated that the psychiatrist acted independently of the hospital, and promised to look further into the genesis of the psychiatrist's behavior. He subsequently told the psychiatrist that income from managed mental health care firms was expected to exceed that of other services and that any rifts to managed care caused by his employees would not be tolerated.

The HMO director informed the psychiatrist that the exclusion from the provider list had nothing to do with any alleged vendetta but was solely the result of the ineligibility of any provider to join the HMO through the health side of the benefit package. He implied that the psychiatrist was out of line and that no such complaints would be entertained in the future. The psychiatrist also heard from the managed mental health care firm of its consideration of a defamation suit against her. In response to these incentives, the psychiatrist issued a written retraction of her remarks as well as an apology both to the medical director and to the executive director of the managed mental health care firm.

CASE ILLUSTRATION 5

A managed mental health care company was invited into a city to take over a contract for capitated business with a 15,000-member HMO plan. A local subsidiary was formed as part of a larger corporate network that extended mainly in the midwestern and eastern regions of the United States. The vice president of this corporation hired a psychologist to be the local executive director, asking her to hire a part-time psychiatrist to serve as medical director. The vice president urged caution in this regard, stating, "Psychiatrists can't be trusted. They are all royal pains in the ass. Let me know who you wish to hire because I want to interview him myself. God knows we don't need any more Napoleons around here."

This particular psychiatric community was new to managed care and organized to protest the presence of the new firm. The psychiatrists formed a subcommittee to look into the clinical practices of the firm, finding them sorely lacking. The subcommittee's report, read at an emergency meeting of the group, recommended that the psychiatrists band together to oppose the new Plan. Another speaker alleged that unfair business practices could be expected once the firm became entrenched into the community. An attorney was retained.

The psychiatrists in this community were not unanimous in their dissent. Several responded positively to the new director's need to hire a medical director. The executive director selected one of these psychiatrists and arranged an interview for him to be grilled by the vice president.

Despite the difficulty of this interview, the psychiatrist was able to alleviate some of the vice president's concerns. The psychiatrist stated that he was aware of dissent among his colleagues in the community but felt that the hostilities would eventually diminish. He stated that he and his colleagues had been on "a real gravy train" from insurance companies for years and that cost-containment techniques were needed before further cutbacks in mental health benefits occurred. The vice president decided to retain this psychiatrist, a Dr. Roberts, for 17 hours of outpatient care per week and to provide him with first refusal on subsequent referrals to the hospital.

Experience with Dr. Roberts indicated that he was indeed skillful in blending not only with managed care guidelines but also with nonmedical practitioners whom the firm employed. His experience served to alleviate some of the anxieties of his colleagues—a process furthered by referrals Dr. Roberts generated to psychiatrists in the community.

Dr. Roberts thanked the executive director for recommending him to the vice president. He also expressed his awareness that the executive director was "the boss" but that he would be happy to pitch in if administrative help was required. This was counterbalanced by bi-weekly calls from the vice president warning the executive director not to provide Dr. Roberts with administrative responsibilities or with any other opportunities to "take over." Dr. Roberts's attitude in this regard, however, belied any need for such concerns; in fact, the executive director was pleased to be able to share administrative duties with him on an increasing basis.

Dr. Roberts was skilled in the management of variable lengths of inpatient stays, and days per thousand in this category rapidly came within the acceptable range established by the corporation. Over time, the managed mental health care firm became known for quality and integrity in its delivery of clinical services. Two years after Dr. Roberts was hired, the vice president began calling him for advice on psychiatric consults and other administrative matters having to do with the national operation of the company. The vice president stated to the executive director his desire to "place clones of Dr. Roberts in every subsidiary in the country." His attitude toward psychiatrists began to soften, and this carried over into other corporate locations around the country.

CASE ILLUSTRATION 6

A psychiatrist, Dr. Fields, had been credentialed to provide inpatient and outpatient services to patients referred by a managed mental health care firm. She had done very good work for the firm, and the local director had been pleased with the quality and the efficiency of her inpatient services.

Unfortunately, however, Dr. Fields's initial work with two inpatients had gone 16 weeks without reimbursement from the Plan. This was in violation of her contract, which stated that uncontested claims would be paid within 30 days of receipt. Dr. Fields contacted the director about this problem. He asked her to write a letter to him, which he would then send along to the corporate office.

Upon receipt of this letter, the director faxed it to the corporate vice president who agreed to look into the matter promptly. The director did not, however, inform Dr. Fields of his actions on her behalf. The vice president faxed back a message that the problem had been identified and that a check had been cut by hand and placed in the mail to Dr. Fields. The director also failed in this instance to inform Dr. Fields of this disposition and so was surprised a month later to hear that she still had not been paid. He apologized to Dr. Fields for his failure to communicate with her adequately and for the failure of his company to resolve the problem more promptly. He then recontacted the vice president who made sure that Dr. Fields was reimbursed via express mail the following day.

The factor that distinguished Dr. Fields from some of her medical and nonmedical colleagues was her patience and civility while attempting to resolve this problem. She did not rant or rave to the director nor did she in any way exceed the boundary of her professional role. She also did not sit back passively month after month as checks allegedly in the mail continued to elude her address. This approach allowed both the local director and the corporate office to more quickly identify a problem not just with Dr. Fields but with the claims process in general. Both parties benefited from the exchange, and the referral relationship continued uninterrupted.

NONMEDICAL PRACTITIONERS

Many of the guidelines that apply to medical practitioners apply as well to nonmedical practitioners except that emphasis shifts from psychopharmacology and inpatient care to the authorization and provision of outpatient services. Managed care firms expect nonmedical practitioners to provide the bulk of outpatient care and to provide it as efficiently and as effectively as possible. Nonmedical clinicians are expected to comply with additional-care review, cooperate with outpatient therapy procedures established by the firm, and stay abreast of relevant research. Some practitioners are more compatible than others with such demands.

The theoretical orientation of a practitioner is of great interest to managed care firms, many of whom are looking toward clinicians who specialize either in behavioral, cognitive-behavioral, or family systems modes of intervention. Measures of clinical outcome are also becoming more sophisticated, and managed care will expect clinicians to be aware of these developments, too (see Chapter 8). The location of practitioners fluent in the new psychotherapies is of paramount importance to managed care firms.

CASE ILLUSTRATION 7

A 130,000-member plan was opening in a major city on the East Coast. A managed mental health care firm had been contracted by an HMO to provide all mental health services. This contract had been transferred from one managed care firm to another, and approximately 2,000 patients were already in care with therapists unconnected with the new HMO.

The firm decided to allow "transition visits" into their developing network. Upon receipt of an acceptable treatment summary, this firm authorized up to eight visits to out of network providers before requiring that clients come back into the network for further care. This policy communicated to the community the firm's emphasis on brief therapy. It also gave the firm an opportunity to observe the quality of the work of community providers.

The executive director of the local Plan, a psychologist, and the vice president of development from the corporate office, met together to review these treatment summaries. In order to diminish paperwork requirements, this firm asked only for the following information on treatment summary reports: patient name, birthdate, and social security number; diagnosis; brief statement of presenting problem; medication status; treatment goals; and treatment plan. It was communicated to providers that only one to two pages of information were required.

The executive director and the vice president were dismayed by the majority of treatment summaries. A representative example is provided below.

Patient: Janice Jones

Social Security Number: 229-80-8514

Birthdate: 2/4/53

Medications: None

Diagnosis: 309.00 Adjustment Disorder With Depressed Mood

Presenting Problem: Ms. Jones presented for treatment four months ago with complaints of depression and sadness following the departure of her daughter for college. Ms. Jones is a widow, and her daughter's departure meant that Ms. Jones is now living alone. There were no vegetative signs or suicidal ideation; however, Ms. Jones did state that life seemed meaningless and that she was not sure how she would be able to cope. She is crying frequently and preoccupied with her daughter's absence. She is continuing to work as a secretary but is not doing much after work or on weekends. I have seen this patient for 20 visits and would like to request the additional 8 visits allowable. If at all possible, I would prefer to see this patient beyond the 8 visits in order to complete her care. I believe that another year of treatment would be applicable in this instance and would prevent this patient from having to undergo the trauma of changing therapists.

Treatment Goals:

1. Provide support for Ms. Jones's loss.
2. Help the patient understand the symbolic loss of her daughter, especially with relation to her early childhood (mother died when patient was 4 years old).
3. Increase the patient's ego strength and ego functioning.
4. Improve the patient's sense of self.
5. Help the patient develop greater insight into the origin of her depression.

Treatment Plan: Interpret the patient's dreams and her verbal material during sessions, with the primary goal of connecting present to past. Provide empathy, warmth, and support. Help the patient get in touch with her inner child. Use transference to aid the patient's working through.

Please advise if I can provide you with any further information or assistance in this regard.

Sincerely,

Janice Boswell, PH.D.
License #551

The information above is fairly typical of treatment summaries presented to managed care companies under such circumstances. Although Dr. Boswell was a therapist in good standing in the community who provided reasonable standards of care, managed care representatives were chagrined with her approach. They noted the emphasis on long-term care; the focus on childhood memories as both the etiology of the problem and the means toward its resolution; treatment goals and terminology that were vague and difficult to define ("ego," "sense of self"), and inadequate empirical validation for recommended interventions.

This therapist was granted the maximum number of transition visits, but the Plan did not proffer her an application to join the developing provider group.

Ms. Jones decided to discontinue treatment with Dr. Boswell and enter care through the new managed care network. She stated that she liked Dr. Boswell very much and appreciated the considerable amount of support received during treatment. Ms. Jones also stated that despite having made progress, she felt "stuck" and wished to try another therapist to see if some additional improvement could be made.

Ms. Jones was referred to another psychologist who confirmed the patient's diagnosis and presenting problem. Included below, however, are the psychologist's goals and treatment plan, which highlight the type of approach often preferred by managed care.

Impression of Etiology: Since additional information has been requested on this patient, please be advised of the following. Although Ms. Jones suffered the loss of her mother when she was 4 years old, I do not believe this to be the primary cause of the problems associated with the patient's loss of her daughter to college. My assessment of this case indicates that Ms. Jones is lacking social intercourse and other sources of pleasure and support in her life. Her social skills are somewhat limited. She does not maintain eye contact, talks mainly about the loss of her daughter, and generally fails to ask questions of others, engage them, or provide them with positive feedback or support. This is consistent with Lewinsohn's conceptualization of individuals who are subject to reactive depressions.

Following the death of her mother, Ms. Jones developed a caretaker role in her family and received little support or praise for this role. Perhaps as a consequence, Ms. Jones has low self-esteem characterized by feelings of inadequacy, which become evident when she talks about the meaning of her daughter's departure. I conduct a structured social skills group, six sessions in duration, which I think will provide Ms. Jones not only with support but also with a chance to improve her social skills so as to develop a better support system in her community. I would also like four to eight additional sessions in order to address the self-esteem issues mentioned above.

Treatment Goals:

1. Increase Ms. Jones's social skills with directive educational intervention.
2. Significantly reduce or eliminate crying episodes.
3. Apply Beck's cognitive restructuring interventions to the client's tendencies toward self-denigration.
4. Reduce the client's score on the Beck's Depression Inventory from 20 (current) to a normal range (0 to 10).
5. Request that the client participate in three pleasurable activities per week.
6. Request that the client join one organization or take one class per quarter.
7. Refer the client to a local women's support group run by paraprofessionals at no charge.

Treatment Plan:

1. Apply Lewinsohn's approach to six sessions of social skills intervention in group.
2. Employ cognitive therapy for depressenogenic cognitions that appear to be affecting client's self-esteem.
3. Ask the client to communicate feelings to her daughter so as to increase their communication.
4. Follow up with social skills and with cognitive/assertiveness homework assignments in order to work toward increasing the client's support system and independence.

The treatment plan above is present oriented, goal directed, measurable (in terms of overt behavior and validated questionnaire scores), and characterized by treatments with clinical outcome superior to placebo and to alternate treatment interventions. (Further information about this type of approach is available in Chapter 8.)

CONTRACTUAL CAVEATS

Since managed mental health care companies differ along many parameters, the practitioner is advised to carefully consider all contractual offers. There have been a number of instances in which providers have been seriously damaged by consenting to disadvantageous arrangements.

A primary concern is the financial stability of the Plan. In some cases, the Plan will disclose financial statements that provide an evaluation of financial stability. Such information can often be obtained from the office of the insurance commissioner. Other indications of financial stability—albeit tenuous—include the age of the Plan (plans 10 years or older tend to be more sound), size (plans of 50,000 or more tend to be more stable), and the success of the plan in its attempts to grow.

Some managed mental health care companies work strictly with HMOs and live or die according to the HMO's ability to sustain itself in the marketplace. Thus, it is also wise to assess, in the manner mentioned above, the financial stability of the HMO. Obtain a copy of the HMO's mental health benefits. One can tell from the benefit package whether the HMO focuses more on inpatient or outpatient care. One can also then assess personal comfort with the coverage provided. (For instance, some providers feel that 20 sessions per calendar year are sufficient; others do not.)

The firm's contract will also provide clues to "provider friendliness." Some contracts do not give adequate protection. Although this does not automatically mean that the provider should avoid the firm, it is most assuredly a bad sign. The following clauses generally should not appear in a contract provided by a reputable firm. If they do appear, the provider should avoid the firm entirely, attempt to negotiate the clause out of the contract before signing it, or seek the advice of an attorney:

1. *"Exclusivity"*: Some managed care contracts require the provider to contract with no other managed care plans. This is obviously a detriment to the provider because of its restriction on the provider's referral base, among other things.
2. *"Overpayment penalty"*: This refers to instances in which the managed care plan inadvertently overpays the provider. An overpayment clause will require the provider to repay the amount plus interest.
3. *"Non-payment for 'Ineligibles'"*: Some Plans refer cases that are actually ineligible for coverage. These may include clients who have dropped the HMO. An ineligible clause exempts the Plan from paying the provider under such circumstances.

4. *"Termination"*: The provider should ensure that the managed care contract can be terminated *without cause* upon no more than 60 to 90 days' written notice. (A 60-day notice is preferable.) Should the managed care relationship turn out to be unfair or unfavorable, this clause allows the provider to endure the negative consequences for a relatively short amount of time.

5. *"Provision of Payment"*: The provider should attempt to ensure that a timely pay period is written into the contract for uncontested claims. Thirty days after receipt is a reasonable target.

6. *"Favored Nations"*: Signature of a contract with this clause guarantees to the managed care firm that the provider will not be undersold. In other words, should the provider offer a 60 percent discount to a special client, the managed care firm, regardless of other contractual stipulations, could require the same discount on all subsequent referrals for care.

7. *"Unlimited Withholds"*: Some managed care firms withhold a certain amount (e.g., 15 percent) of provider reimbursements into a pool that is redistributed to providers only under conditions of profitability or acceptable costs for services. This arrangement is most typical among Independent Practitioner Associations that contract on members' behalves with managed care firms. If withholds are unspecified, the managed care firm could, theoretically, deny all reimbursements under conditions of extreme financial loss.*

Should a managed mental health care firm become insolvent, the provider will face a difficult dilemma, especially if the provider is carrying a number of patients formerly covered by the firm. The inability of a patient to pay under such circumstances does not release the provider from responsibility for the patient's care (see Chapter 9). Although most of this chapter counseled providers to approach managed care with an open mind, it is still wise to determine whether each particular company is disreputable or prone toward business practices that put the therapist at risk. Such practices are of course intolerable and not to be condoned.

---

* The author is indebted to Nancy Brace (Brace, 1990) for permission to paraphrase excerpts from her paper on HMO contracting.

Chapter 5

Mental Health Care Benefits: A Guide to Purchase and Management

Cost-containment efforts have divided into a dizzying variety of service delivery options. Some employers have completely deleted all mental health benefits. Others have relied on governmental intervention to reduce the costs of care. In between these extremes are solutions for the organization of health care benefits into service delivery systems ranging from relatively "loose" preferred practitioner organizations (PPOs) to more highly constrained HMOs. These options can be confusing to those in administrative positions charged with the responsibility of corporate health care costs. Mental health care tends to be especially bewildering. This chapter provides clarification of these questions and concerns.

SHOULD MENTAL HEALTH BENEFITS BE EXCLUDED FROM COVERAGE?

Mental health has been covered to a lesser extent than other health care services. Initial surveys indicated that especially high users of psychological treatment were therapists themselves. This, in combination with the emergence of therapies primarily aimed at self-actualization or personal growth, led insurers to the impression that mental health services were largely unnecessary or superfluous, used primarily by the "worried well" or by patients whose disturbances were otherwise mild or insignificant.

The mental health stigma—its focus on deeply personal, and sometimes mystifying concerns—influenced coverage deemphasis. Also contributing was the restricted range of diagnoses submitted by outpatient therapists to insurance carriers. Many of these reflected benign conditions, inadvertently strengthening the position that mental health services were superfluous. Ironically, the predominance of mild diagnoses instead reflected clinician biases toward protecting the patient (e.g., Sharfstein, 1978).

A survey of small companies in Denver with administrative services only (ASO) accounts (see later in this chapter) indicated that a significant percentage offered extremely limited mental health coverage (Giles, 1989). A typical benefit package included five or fewer outpatient visits per calendar year with even more limited care for inpatient treatment. The health care benefits for these companies were not nearly so constrained. Adversaries of managed mental health care would do well to note this disturbing trend: Some managers are reacting to rising costs by cutting these benefits entirely. From a perspective of human need, the exclusion of mental health care benefits is unfortunate because the concerns noted above are unfounded (i.e., the majority of outpatient services are provided to individuals who are moderately to severely disabled [e.g., Sharfstein & Taube, 1982]).

Practitioners chafe at the suggestion that mental health conditions are insignificant. On a not atypical day as director of a managed care facility, the author saw an inpatient who had attempted to hack himself to death with a butcher knife; a woman who had just failed in her twenty-sixth attempt to commit suicide; and a gentleman who had survived, surprisingly intact, the self-infliction of a bullet wound through his brain. Although these patients required inpatient care, they did not stay in the hospital forever and they eventually needed treatment on an outpatient basis. On another day, the author saw a client who spent four hours on daily washing rituals before leaving home, another who was housebound with panic attacks and could only make it to treatment when accompanied by her spouse, a young woman spending at least $350 a week on junk food that she consumed and subsequently regurgitated, and a gentleman who was too lethargic from depression to go to work. Outpatient practitioners regularly face such difficulties. Divorces, deaths, and losses of position, while not necessarily leading to severe psychiatric disorders, may still entail considerable emotional disturbance and very legitimate need for care.

Managed mental health care companies administering and delivering HMO benefits are typically directed by benefit packages to exclude conditions that do not meet formal psychiatric diagnoses in the DSM-III-R. (These usually include codes and treatments aimed solely at autonomy or personal growth.) Despite fiscal motivation to detect and exclude such requests for care, the incidence of exclusion is less than 1 case in 200 (MCC Cos., unpublished data). Such observations provide further indication that outpatient services are directed toward legitimate human needs.

If one accedes to the argument that mental health benefits are not wasted luxuries directed toward trivial conditions, one must still face the reality that health care benefits can no longer be provided from a bottomless fiscal well. Certain benefits must be cut. Certain services must be sacrificed or carefully rationed. It is in this context that mental health services appear to be particularly resilient because their inclusion provides a measure of containment of health care costs. This appears to be due primarily to two mental health treatment effects. The first is the reduction of "performance costs" such as absenteeism, turnover, and impaired production. This phenomenon is discussed later in this chapter. The second source of savings is from the "medical cost offset effect," addressed here.

Cost offset refers to a diverse series of studies, conducted across a range of medical and psychiatric problems, indicating that the provision of mental health services reduces health care expense. Cost reductions are often in excess of the initial expense for mental health treatment.

The first major review on this question found that medical services significantly decreased subsequent to the initiation of psychotherapeutic intervention (Jones & Vischi, 1979). In 12 of 13 studies these authors found service reductions ranging from 5 to 85 percent.

Mumford, Schlesinger, and Glass (1982) found that psychotherapy helped patients recover from surgery for heart attacks an average of two days more quickly than a control group who received no such attention. Mumford, Schlesinger, Glass, Patrick, and Cuerdon (1984) performed a meta-analysis on 58 studies of medical utilization following psychotherapy. Decreases in medical use following psychological intervention were reported in 85 percent of these studies.

The subset of studies in this group using naturalistic (unrandomized) experimental designs yielded an average cost effect size of 33.1 percent. The studies using randomization yielded a lower percent change (10.4 percent), but cost reductions were still significant. Approximately three-quarters of this effect are due to the subsequent decrease in need for medical hospitalization (versus outpatient visits to the physician). Savings for patients 55 years of age and older tend to be maximized by psychotherapeutic interventions. These results have been replicated by other research teams (e.g., Sloan & Chmel, 1991).

Holder and Blose (1987) showed that those who receive mental health treatment also incur higher medical costs on a pretreatment basis. However, these costs dropped significantly after the initiation of psychotherapy and continued to decline over the study period of three years. Older subjects had the largest offsets.

Offset effects also follow treatment for chemical dependency. For example, one year prior to care, alcoholics incur 100 percent more costs for health services than do normal controls. This figure may increase as much as 200 to 300 percent for the 12- to 24-month period prior to receipt of substance abuse care (Holder, 1987). Jones and Vischi (1979) found a 26 to 69 percent reduction in health costs following chemical dependency treatment. This represented a savings of $1.10 for each $1 invested.

Once alcoholism treatment is initiated, subsequent medical costs begin a downward trend, which continues into the fourth and fifth year posttreatment (Holder, 1987). As will be reviewed in later chapters, substance abuse treatment seems highly subject to dose paradox: Intensive inpatient treatment does not typically yield better outcome than outpatient care. The cost offset effects reported above are conservative since the majority of reports studied inpatient use.

Cost offset effects indicate that mental health services address substantial public need and reduce costs sufficiently to pay for or exceed initial expense. The answer to our first question—Should mental health benefits be excluded from coverage?—is no, in most cases.

The potential of the cost offset effect has just begun to be explored. In fact, mental health services may hold the key to an effective solution to the health care crisis. In 1984, the results of the Carter Center study (Amler & Duhl, 1984) on health care pointed to the startling conclusion that many health care expenditures are preventable. The Carter Center study indicated that diseases are often attributable to causes that are primarily "lifestyle" in nature.

The study examined 14 high-priority health problems. Selection was based on five criteria: (1) point prevalence and secular trends, (2) severity in terms of health impact and cost, (3) sensitivity to intervention using current scientific or operational knowledge, (4) feasibility of intervention, and (5) generic applicability of intervention to other health problems.

These 14 health problems accounted for nearly 70 percent of hospital days, 85 percent of direct personal health care expenditures, 80 percent of deaths, and 90 percent of potential years of life lost before age 65 years in the United States in 1980. Roughly two-thirds of reported mortality were due to potentially preventable causes—1.2 million deaths (65 percent) and 8.4 million years lost before age 65 years (63 percent). Tobacco use was the leading generic risk associated with mortality. Other risk factors associated with premature death were high blood pressure, improper nutrition, and lack of preventive medical screening. Alcohol overuse was also a principal cause of premature mortality.

According to the Carter Center study, tobacco use causes more than 1,000 unnecessary deaths every day. These usually occur as cardiovascular problems (heart attacks, strokes, and complications of diabetes, cancer, and lung disease). Tobacco also accounts for a significant degree of infant mortality, deaths due to house fires, peptic ulcer disease, and vascular disease.

Alcohol was found to be the second leading cause of premature death. One-third of the loss is due to automobile fatalities, one-third to other injuries such as fire or drowning, and the remaining one-third includes violence, cirrhosis, and cancer of the mouth, larynx, and esophagus.

The Carter Center study showed that unwanted pregnancies (which account for 55 percent of all pregnancies in the United States) and mental health problems—especially depression, substance abuse, and violence—are extremely important contributors to premature death and inflated health costs. Many of these problems are preventable without need to rely on new or expensive technology. These findings point to prevention in lowering health care costs—the mission that HMOs were originally developed to pursue. HMOs as well as indemnity insurers have substantially deviated from this mission, relying instead on tertiary prevention strategies for health care.

The Carter Center study has not attracted the attention it deserves. One of the most significant of its consequences is a book by Sloan and Chmel (1991), *The Quality Revolution and Health Care: A Primer for Purchasers and Providers*. These authors expanded on the Carter Center results with references to literature that 50 percent or more of outpatient visits to physicians are actually mental health in nature. They cite research reporting that physicians do not readily detect emotional disturbances, leading to chronic outpatient or inpatient medical care for problems that could be better, and more cheaply, handled by psychotherapists. Sloan and Chmel presented data complimenting the Carter Center's indications that the genesis of illness is often from preventable causes of a behavioral nature. They proposed a "manufacturing model" of health care based on the quality literature (e.g., Deming, 1988) subsequently adopted to manufacturing and administration models by the Japanese.

Sloan and Chmel criticized cost-containment techniques, indicating that dramatic cost *reductions* in the present system are possible by prevention, proper diagnosis and treatment of emotional concerns "somaticizing" into masks for physical disease, early identification and treatment of substance abuse, a view of hospitalization as a defect in the "manufacture" of health, and behavioral tracking procedures for use in preventing inpatient treatment of chronic disease. These provocative concepts await further evaluation.

WHAT SHOULD MENTAL HEALTH BENEFITS BE?

The cost and structure of mental health care benefits is an extremely complicated question; however, certain concepts generally apply. The following benefits recommendations will, when satisfactorily managed, be adequate to meet the majority of cases of need.

The first factor of interest is that of benefit limitation and cost shifting. Available research indicates that patient contribution to health costs influences subsequent utilization (Manning, Wells, & Benjamin, 1987). As expected, the more the patient has to pay, the less use is observed. The dilemma occurs with regard to choosing amounts that prevent moral hazard while maintaining appropriate access.

The downside of increased copays and deductibles is that they do not seem to discriminate effective from inadequate care. From a managed mental health care perspective, assuming that the only necessary mental health care was that serious enough to warrant hospitalization, traditional indemnity plans had benefits' incentives backward. Modern benefit plans are structured so that patient contribution increases for inpatient care while decreasing for outpatient care.

Federally qualified HMOs, and some other types of insurance options, are regulated by changing state and/or federal legislation mandating minimum levels of mental health benefits. (Currently these mandates can be bypassed by self-funded employers—see the discussion of ASOs later in this chapter). A typical mandate includes 20 outpatient visits per calendar year and 30 to 45 days per calendar year of inpatient care. Sometimes the copayments are variable under the law. If so, a copay of not less than $15 and not more than $30 per outpatient visit is recommended. Higher copayments for outpatient care provide less opportunity for problems to be assessed in time for inpatient treatment to be prevented. State mandates for inpatient care will sometimes include low deductibles (e.g., $100 to $200 per admission), which tend to influence higher than expected admissions per thousand. Where possible, some insurance companies opt for a patient copay of a percentage of the total bill, commonly 20 percent. Another option is to establish a set fee (e.g., $50) for an inpatient day. Because these copayment amounts are fairly substantial, they tend to limit moral hazard for inappropriate admissions and excessive lengths of stay.

A drawback of these conditions, however, is their susceptibility to manipulation. In order to persuade a member to seek hospitalization, these copayments are sometimes waived by hospital personnel. This increases moral hazard for both the provider and the consumer, raising costs of mental health care considerably. Counterregulatory efforts are easily circumvented, and their violation is difficult to prove. This is another indication for care management: Managed care companies negotiate set per diem fees that do not vary by patient copay. This also prevents the hospital from adding ancillary charges to compensate for missing patient copays. Preadmission certification prevents inappropriate admissions regardless of prior deals made by patient and hospital. Employers and insurance plans failing to utilize these procedures are open to abuse.

The A. Foster Higgins report referred to in Chapter 4 (Foster Higgins & Co., 1989) indicated that 87 percent of employer respondents limited inpatient benefits, up from 75 percent in 1988. The limitations included lifetime and annual benefit limits (or "caps") and the imposition of maximums on numbers of days covered for inpatient care. This cost-containment strategy, *in lieu of actual managed care,* proved to be effective. One or more such limitations were associated with an average cost of $230 per employee (annualized), 18.4 percent less than the $282 incurred by employees covered under less restrictive mental health policies.

The report went on to indicate that the most successful cost-containment strategy was the imposition of an annual dollar limit on inpatient care both for mental health and substance abuse benefits. Employers utilizing these annual limits reported per-employee costs of $199 in 1989, 24.3 percent less than the $263 reported by employers who did not impose such limits. The median cap among policies was $10,000 per year.

The Foster Higgins report warned that annual dollar limits should not be set too low:

> In setting a maximum, employers should carefully consider what amount will still provide employees with adequate coverage. In most parts of the country, a $10,000 maximum will pay for 21 days of inpatient care, which will not cover the standard 28-day substance abuse programs and may not be enough to treat acute mental illness. (*Business Insurance*, December 3, 1990, pp. 2–3)

Although this advice is sound as far as it goes, it indicates that cost inflation may be expected for companies whose mental health care benefits are not managed well. Employees needing substance abuse care in managed settings rarely receive 28 days of rehabilitation. The average length of stay is 3 to 5 days, and the majority of treatment is rendered on an outpatient basis.

Lifetime maximums, usually $50,000, were less effective in reducing benefits in the short run. Costs for plans with lifetime caps were $227 per employee, or 6.2 percent less than the $242 noted for employees covered by plans without such a limitation. Lifetime maximums have little impact on employers suffering from high employee turnover.

The survey also found that about half of employers limit the number of covered days for inpatient treatment per benefit period, typically one year. The most common limitation (41 percent of employers) was a 30-day maximum inpatient stay per calendar year. Interestingly, the cost of mental health and substance abuse was approximately the same for employers limiting the number of inpatient days per year in comparison with employers who did not. While this was surprising to several reviewers of the study, it was not surprising to managed mental health care representatives: The maximum number of available inpatient days will tend to be utilized unless concurrent stay review is in place. A 30-day maximum, unless managed, will typically—and sometimes inappropriately—mean a 30 day course of inpatient care.

Several other points of concern can be noted from this important survey. Only one-third of respondents screened at least some of their employees for substance abuse as part of the preemployment process. Although this is up from 24 percent reported in 1988, it still indicates a rather widespread lack of knowledge about the true costs of substance-abusing employees.

Only 9 percent of employers indicated that they provided utilization review programs for inpatient mental health and substance abuse treatment, and only 6 percent had separate utilization review programs for outpatient treatment. Finally, only 5 percent of respondents indicated that they employed a managed mental health care operation for their mental health and substance abuse benefits. From a managed care perspective, the great majority of employers are thus spending a great deal more than necessary for their mental health benefits.

HOW SHOULD MENTAL HEALTH BENEFITS BE DELIVERED?

The question of service delivery brings about managed care options. The following subcategories proceed in the order of increasing management of mental health benefits and care.

Employee Assistance Programs

Employee Assistance Programs (EAPs) were originally developed to enhance the accurate and timely capture of alcohol-dependent employees in order to arrange for their care. EAP clinicians were often recovering themselves and typically directed treatment toward 28-day inpatient detoxification/rehabilitation programs. As an aside, it is interesting to note that the 28-day rehabilitation was chosen because 28 days comprised the standard shore leave of Navy personnel (Mines, 1990).

The primary concept behind EAP work is that troubled employees cause excess absenteeism, turnover, and poor productivity. A lack of timely detection of such problems may lead to significant difficulties in the work force.

EAPs are not often mentioned as part of health care networks and are inadequately referenced as part of managed systems. Despite this, the role of the EAP in managed mental health care should not be underestimated. In and of themselves, EAPs are a form of managed care. The form and mission of the EAP in managed care, however, can be very different from that which is recommended in this book. Herein lies the potential both for problems and solutions within the new managed networks.

Nearly two-thirds of *Fortune 500* companies employ EAPs (Jansen, 1986). Initial reports on EAP effectiveness have been very encouraging. Firestone Tire and Rubber, for instance, estimated EAP savings of $1.7 million, or $2,350 per person involved, after one year of operation. United Airlines reported a return of $16.35 for each dollar invested in EAP costs (Jansen, 1986). Corporate executives often associate EAPs with improved employee morale and job satisfaction. Properly run EAPs might also have significant influence on medical cost offset effects (discussed in the previous section). It should be noted, however, that many of the reports on EAPs have come from naturalistic studies or studies that were otherwise plagued by methodological problems that shed caution on results. As seen in the prior section, the estimate of medical offset effects, while still significant, decreased considerably with studies using more adequate methodological controls.

Like managed care in general, EAPs vary greatly. Their services are diverse and their counselors trained in many different forms of clinical practice and philosophy. The competence of an EAP program may be further complicated by the values used to evaluate its effectiveness. In this context, the same EAP program might be judged superior by one standard yet disastrous by another. Standards determined by managed care philosophy often assess critically the performance of the traditional EAP.

In a sense, EAP professionals are contracted by employers to increase utilization of mental health or substance abuse services. The EAP professional is mandated to train supervisors to recognize problem employees. Bulletins, announcements, and other indications of EAP services are broadly published and distributed to employees. The EAP is often "in house" or has some other means of securing that access to services is readily available.

EAPs work on an *assessment and referral model*, leaving extended treatment to members of an external provider network. The EAP usually establishes an informal network of inpatient and outpatient facilities to whom employees are referred. There is often an emphasis on inpatient treatment. (Again, EAP programs vary tremendously along the lines of restricted or unrestrictive therapeutic environments. More traditional EAPs tend toward longer-term inpatient and outpatient treatment. This trend, however, is changing.) EAP professionals often have substantial influence in their companies and in their communities, and their control of referral business makes them important to private outpatient and inpatient practitioners.

Although EAPs provide a very important function, support for them should be rendered in a discriminative fashion. From a cost-containment perspective, the best EAPs coordinate well with a managed mental health care system. Obtaining this coordination is not always easy, however .

Since the primary EAP function is to detect emotional, legal, and vocational concerns of employees (and thereby to increase utilization), the EAP professional is often set on a collision course with managed care systems. EAP conflicts with managed care are common, and a substantial literature about this has been developing over the last 10 years. Much of this literature indicates that employers play a role in setting up such problems.

It is extremely important that employers who choose an EAP know beforehand what they are hiring the EAP to accomplish. A general philosophy of practice as well as a specific job description and mission are invaluable for giving the EAP proper guidance. Traditional EAP professionals, working in the manner in which they were trained, will be upset by the intrusion of a managed care firm that the employer brings on to contain costs.

This situation invokes understandable confusion to the EAP. Without formal guidance, a traditional EAP program director will assume that he or she is doing a good job by increasing utilization to "acceptable" levels—a typical target is 5 to 10 percent of the employee base. As the EAP does a good job, however, mental health costs tend to rise considerably. An employer having inadequate knowledge about the reasons for cost escalation will not be aware of the mixed message sent to the EAP by hiring a managed care service. In this instance, the EAP professional will begin to feel subtly reprimanded. If the job has been done well, the reasoning goes, then why has managed care been asked to take over some of the EAP functions? Few employers foresee the disruption that subsequently ensues.

EAP programs involve service benefits that have varying intensities of availability and costs. The EAP principally ensures that referrals are followed up and that competent treatment is provided. The EAP professional will often follow an employee's care through an outpatient course of treatment or through a stay on a psychiatric or substance abuse unit. In general, the EAP is an employee advocate, and many professionals take to this role with an impressive sense of sincerity. At the same time, it is sometimes hard for such individuals to accept what they feel is a compromise in care when a managed company begins operations. Thus, the employer cannot leave EAP and managed care in the same room with the unqualified assumption that they will get along. Both must be apprised of the mission of the company and requested—firmly—to work together for the common good.

Sometimes an employer is worried about high absenteeism or turnover rates and is less concerned about the actual costs of the provision of subsequent mental health benefits. In such cases, a traditional EAP program will be sufficient, and no managed care variant will be necessary. It should be noted, however, that some EAP programs are becoming more sophisticated in managed care techniques. Such EAP programs are developing a philosophy compatible with least restrictive therapeutic environments, brief therapies, and preadmission and concurrent stay reviews. All else being equal, for the sake of future expenditures, the employer would be wise to hire the services of this latter type of EAP.

From 25 to 66 percent of all absences are emotional in nature. An average of $3,000 is needed to train clerical employees, and executive training can run into the tens of thousands of dollars (Jansen, 1986). A functional EAP can probably reduce these problems and may also be able to increase productivity and satisfaction among workers.

A study of the McDonnell Douglas EAP was conducted by the Alexander and Alexander consulting group (Smith & Mahoney, 1990). The study involved 25,000 employees from 1985 through 1989. Analysis of medical claims allowed the identification of employees who had been treated for mental health or substance abuse problems. Some of these employees elected to see the EAP and some did not. Some were covered by HMO plans, others were covered by indemnity plans. Finally, there was a control group, used for comparison purposes, of employees with no mental health or substance abuse claims. Unfortunately, this study suffers from lack of randomization. Its results, though encouraging, might be due either to the intervention of the EAP or to sample (or other) biases introduced by its naturalistic design.

This report replicated prior indications that employees suffering with serious substance abuse or mental health problems are very expensive to maintain. For example, chemically dependent employees lost an average of 28 excess days to absenteeism per year during the five years of the study. Employees treated for mental illness incurred an average of 14 excess days of absenteeism per year.

Four years after treatment, 55 percent of the McDonnell Douglas employees treated for substance abuse were no longer employed by the company; 23 percent of employees with psychiatric conditions also lost their jobs. During the study period, claims payment excesses for health care were $23,000 for substance abusers and $13,000 for employees suffering with mental illness. Additional costs were incurred for medical services among the dependents of chemically dependent or psychiatrically ill employees.

These results indicate, as is common, that McDonnell Douglas paid insufficient attention to employee screening processes during hiring periods. The group of EAP clients treated for chemical dependencies lost 29 percent fewer days over the study period than did employees treated outside of EAP contact. Similarly, a 25 percent reduction in lost days was found for EAP clients treated for psychiatric conditions. Some 32 percent of EAP clients treated for substance abuse had been terminated or had quit their positions at the end of the 5 years (versus 55 percent overall). There was a 28 percent drop for psychiatric conditions in this category.

A significant medical cost offset effect was also found in this study. For example, during the five-year period, EAP clients treated for substance abuse incurred about $7,000 less in medical claims than did substance abusing employees who did not use the EAP. (Psychiatric costs were $4,000 lower). Similar effects were found for dependents. For reasons unexplained in the study, EAP cases covered by HMOs generally showed poorer results, especially with turnover, than employees covered by more traditional insurance options. Due to study flaws, these results cannot be directly attributed to the EAP itself. They do, however, add to the existing literature suggesting positive effects.

Many employers would be wise to consider the addition of an EAP program to existing services; however, EAP programs cannot be expected to negotiate maximally favorable hospital contracts. Their contingent of employees is not always large enough to command significant inpatient discounts. Since the EAP mandate is for service provision, there may be less emphasis on cost-containment techniques (brief treatments, outpatient versus inpatient services, and various aspects of utilization review).

The author has had contact with a number of EAP professionals who acquired impressive knowledge of, and compatibility with, managed care. These professionals had expertise with case management, hospital utilization review, and least restrictive treatment environments. Nevertheless, due in large measure to the factors previously discussed, the additional institution of managed mental health care resulted in cost savings of 30 to 70 percent.

The A. Foster Higgins survey found that employers with EAPs spent $272 per employee in 1989 for mental health costs, 36 percent more than the $200 spent by employers without EAPs. According to the survey, "Given that a primary function of EAPs has been to refer employees to mental health care providers, it is not surprising that they tend to increase utilization." EAP clients in the McDonnell Douglas study incurred greater absenteeism when treated for substance abuse both within the treatment year and the immediate year thereafter. This type of result usually reflects an EAP emphasis upon long-term, inpatient care, made worse by the inability of the EAP to negotiate significant per diem discounts.

An EAP may well be a necessary and extremely valuable adjunct to a comprehensive cost-containment plan. It is seldom sufficient, however. Managed care companies have substantially more experience with cost-containment techniques and can usually bring greater negotiating power to the table when discussing hospital contracts. EAP professionals, again with some exception, are trained primarily in assessment and referral models and cannot maintain operations equivalent to those observed from managed care firms. It would be unreasonable to expect otherwise.

Preferred Practitioner Organizations

A *preferred practitioner organization (PPO)* is a plan that either restricts services to a set list of providers (the exclusive provider organization, or EPO) or provides a fiscal incentive for members to obtain treatment from the providers who have been formally approved. This holds for mental health PPOs as well. Clinicians who get accepted on the list provide discounted fee-for-service treatment to enrollees. When a company extends a contract bid for a PPO, all other things being equal, the PPO giving the greatest discount will be selected. In addition to price, clinicians may be selected based on expectations of efficient treatment. Some PPOs have advanced to a point where provider utilization can be tracked, and "outlier" therapists may be required to alter patterns of practice. The payer's role in negotiating discounts and in demanding that providers comply with utilization review distinguishes PPOs from traditional indemnity plans (Davis et al., 1990). PPOs are sponsored by providers or their representatives. Only 2 percent of self-insured employers sponsored PPOs in 1986 (American Medical Care Review Association, 1986).

PPOs enjoy popularity among enrollees, especially those having "flex" options allowing freedom of choice (albeit at a higher price for out-of-network providers). PPOs with outpatient and inpatient contracts provide some measure of security that in-network facilities are not over-charging in order to make up for lost revenues from Medicare and Medicaid. As indicated by the explosive PPO growth, these types of arrangements tend to be welcomed by providers as well, especially when PPOs fulfill their mission of increasing referrals to members of the provider group. As the PPO grows, members of the list enjoy a larger contingent of enrollees from which to receive referral business.

Although the discounted-service PPO is preferred among mental health clinicians, its fee-for-service structure still provides a financial reward for high use. This type of incentive has been a major part of the problem with escalating costs. Rigorous utilization review procedures may be required to monitor providers and to prevent service abuses in PPO systems.

PPOs are not regulated by the federal government, and so the ade-quacy of their financial reserves, among other things, may not be guaran-teed. (States may regulate PPOs when sponsored by insurance companies or when PPOs assume a financial risk. Some states have passed legislation affecting PPOs, but federal regulations apply only in cases where PPOs grow large enough to incur antitrust concerns.)

Davis, Anderson, Rowland, and Steinberg (1990) reported 73 PPO plans in the country in 1983, compared to 575 in 1988. Enrollment grew from 1.3 million in 1984 to 35 million by 1988. Employers in the A. Foster Higgins survey indicated that PPOs were effective in reducing health costs (although savings averaged only 3.3 percent). There was no infor-mation with regard to the effectiveness of PPOs in reducing mental health care costs.

The flexibility of point-of-service options with PPOs, even when cost sharing with consumers is involved, invites higher use. Out-of-net-work providers are, by definition, unmanaged. Mental health PPOs are at present behind their HMO counterparts with regard to the develop-ment and implementation of cost-containment techniques, management information systems, and formal measures to regulate or ensure quality of care. They typically have less capacity to centrally monitor the com-plete range of inpatient and outpatient services. Since providers are not at financial risk for services, utilization with such plans, and subsequent costs, tend to rise.

Health Maintenance Organizations

Health Maintenance Organizations (HMOs) provide, on a contractual basis, a stated range of health and mental health care services to a voluntarily enrolled population. The HMO accepts a prepayment for services that varies predominantly by the size of the membership. HMOs, or their provider-designees, deliver services under a capitated umbrella: This provides at once both a minimum and maximum amount of incoming revenue to the provider group. If utilization escalates or if treatment extends, the provider group has no fiscal recourse for recovering the difference.

Mental health HMOs are the "major league" of managed mental health care delivery systems. If they underbid capitation, manage care inefficiently, fail to drive appropriate services to outpatient care, or fall prey to a myriad of other pitfalls, they may suffer major financial losses in relatively short periods of time.

Mental health HMOs encounter significant pressure from all sides. Consumers pressure them to enlarge provider lists to increase freedom of choice. Out-of-network providers pressure the HMO for membership; those who are in the network provide various forms of resistance to the extensive regulation that HMO systems employ. Hospitals want higher per diems, greater flexibility to add ancillary charges, or exclusive capture of all enrollees in need. While demanding significantly lower expenditures, employers and insurers also demand that the HMO keep complaints down, ensure that enrollees are reasonably satisfied, and provide high-quality care. Due in part to the nature of capitation itself, these and other interfacing systems—including the state insurance commission and the state legislature—warily monitor the possibility that the mental health HMOs will inappropriately restrain or deny care.

The HMO concept was incorporated into federal legislation via the Health Maintenance Act of 1973 (PL 93–222). Major provisions of this legislation include:

1. That HMOs provide programs for resolution of grievances, quality assurance, and enrollee representation for policy making
2. That enrollees be allowed to participate regardless of current or prior health status and without prejudice according to age, income, or social norms
3. That HMOs meet financial requirements to assure their fiscal solvency
4. That basic health services are offered, including inpatient and outpatient hospital care, physician and emergency services, mental health treatment, diagnostic services, and preventive services

5. That HMOs price benefit packages according to community—versus experience—rating and that employers with 25 or more employees offer an HMO option if requested by a federally qualified HMO in the area. (This law will probably become more comprehensive following congressional revision.)

HMOS are classified according to the manner in which physician services are organized and reimbursed. *Staff model HMOs* employ clinicians on a full-time basis, including mental health staff. In this instance the clinicians are not at risk personally. Health and mental health plans with this type of organization seek to provide very comprehensive services and to provide them, as much as possible, on an exclusively internal basis. The Cigna Health Plan of California, with 450,000 enrollees (as of March, 1988), is the nation's largest staff model (Davis et al., 1990).

Group model HMOs are structured so that the HMO provides the facility and administrative/nonclinical staff but then contracts with one multispecialty group practice for health and/or mental health services. The clinician group is paid a monthly capitation by the HMO for each covered life. Unlike the staff model, the group model offers the clinician group the opportunity to participate in profit-sharing arrangements with the HMO.

Network model HMOs are free to contract with more than one clinician group. In this model, HMOs do not supply facilities or support personnel, arranging by larger capitation payments for the clinician group to provide these services. The network of providers is free to contract with other plans.

The *Individual Practice Association (IPA)* is the fourth category of HMO model. In contrast to networks, the IPA model HMO subcontracts with solo practitioners and/or multispecialty group practices. Sometimes this is arranged through an umbrella contract with a local physician association which then organizes individual clinicians. Solo practitioners are free to accept other fee-for-service or managed care business.

Because HMOs were initially identified as the "heavy hitters" of managed care and subsequently mandated with the goal of containing health costs, much scrutiny has been directed to HMO performance as national membership continues to grow. Much of the relevant literature indicates that HMOs have a positive impact on cost. Luft (1981) found that HMOs, in six consecutive studies, lowered annual cost per person between 10 and 40 percent in comparison to non-HMO plans. The Rand Corporation study indicated that HMO members incurred 25 percent lower expenditures than did enrollees in the fee-for-service options (Lohr, Brook, Kamberg, Goldberg, Leibowitz, Keesey, Reboussin, & Newhouse, 1986). Hospital days were 830 per 1,000 for fee-for-service members versus 490 days per 1,000 for HMOs. This finding was essentially replicated by the Group Health Association of America (GHAA) study (1988). Reduction of inpatient use is primarily responsible for HMO cost containment. This effect is due in large measure to the effect of HMOs on discretionary surgery (e.g., Siu, Leibowitz, Brook, Goldman, Lurie, & Newhouse, 1988).

Despite these positive results, HMO premiums have continued to rise, in most cases only a bit less quickly than those of fee-for-service plans (Davis et al., 1990). To say the least, this has been a source of disgruntlement among payers. The absence of deductibles and the reduced copayments for health care, while lowering costs to patients, have not led to significant cost reductions that could be passed on to employers. The federally qualified HMO must offer a range of benefits that may be more comprehensive and require such minimum cost sharing that premiums continue to soar.

Employers who are unsophisticated in HMO price negotiations are often unaware of ways in which HMOs inflate costs in order to increase profit. The *community rating system*, with which HMOs are mandated to comply, can often be varied more to fit a particular employer than the HMO administrator indicates. HMOs have been found guilty of "shadow pricing"—that is, pricing products just enough lower than fee-for-service business to get the contract but not low enough to reflect actual costs.

HMOs have not been readily available in rural areas nor widely implemented by employers with small numbers of employees. To some extent this is due to lack of HMO interest in small employer groups. (This is probably a poor business practice and one likely to change; TPF&C, 1990).

The use of certain underwriting practices (e.g., the exclusion of high-risk clients or groups) and experience rating allow indemnity plans to bid competitively against HMOs for small business accounts. Indemnity plans are able to take better advantage of claims "lag" (premiums are collected for months before many claims come in). Claims continue to lag collections for the first one to three years following onset of an indemnity plan (TPF&C, 1990). Indemnity insurers are well aware of this effect and can price accordingly. This has also served to shut HMOs out of small business markets, representing another disadvantage of the HMOs.

One of the most successful aspects of managed health care has been managed *mental* health care—such care delivered under an HMO model will typically consume only 3 to 4 percent of the premium (see sections below). Again, however, savings earned by managed mental health care companies are not necessarily passed on to purchasers. These and other factors have caused a number of employers to dislike HMOs and to cause HMO reviewers to indicate that such systems have been only partially successful in their mission to contain costs (Davis et al., 1990).

Administrative Services Only

Administrative services only (ASO) plans are applicable to employers who, noting the disadvantages of the managed care systems discussed above, choose to self-fund their own insurance plans. In this case, the employer buys administrative services, such as claims payments and claims processing, from an existing insurance company. Funding for claims themselves, however, is provided by the employer.

Because of the huge financial risk involved in this strategy, only very large employers (e.g., Chrysler) have been able to rely entirely on ASOs (Califano, 1986). With smaller companies, one especially difficult and expensive case (e.g., the premature birth of a 2-pound infant) can bankrupt the company or severely deplete its operating revenues. Several recent developments, however, make the ASO option more feasible.

With the help of a consultant, an employer who wishes to self-insure can request that a managed care company design a personalized variant of an HMO. At present, self-insureds taking this option bypass the strict regulatory requirements of the HMO Act for federally insured HMOs. The employer can then adopt a number of effective strategies for containing health care costs. These include increased cost sharing for the HMO product; annual and lifetime dollar limits similar to those discussed earlier (these automatically set a limit on employer risk); and the ability to hire a managed mental health care company to provide benefits. This latter option is known as a *carve out* of mental health care. If the employer makes a wise choice, subsequent savings may be substantial. This strategy has the added advantage of management information systems (MIS) reporting capability—provided by managed mental health care corporations—which serve to track in detail the major sources of expenditure for mental health care needs. Additional information on ASOs is available in Kohn, Ondasik, and Repko (1990).

WHAT DO MANAGED MENTAL HEALTH CARE BENEFITS COST?

The answer to this question depends on a number of factors, including geographical location, skill of the parties negotiating benefits, and the cost to the managed mental health care company of doing business in the community. Such factors are entered into a cap calculator, and a price is subsequently derived. Specifics that are entered into the calculator include inpatient per diems both for mental health and substance abuse; costs per internal and external session to provide outpatient care; expected utilization of services on both an outpatient and an inpatient basis; the amount of copayment and coinsurance charges; cost of overhead such as lease, phone, furnishings, equipment, utilities, and supplies; necessary clerical or other support staff; other general and administrative expense; the actual mental health benefits available to members; corporate overhead; and expected profit.

Given the wide variability of many of these factors, it is impossible to provide a blanket price that employers can expect. A range between $2.75 and $6.00 per member per month, however, will capture the majority of employer groups. For these and other reasons, it is imperative that employers bring data on mental health costs and utilization rates to the bargaining table when considering a carve out for managed mental health care. If the managed mental health care company cannot promise significant decreases in price while ensuring quality of care, then the effort is hardly worthwhile.

Point-of-purchase options for such systems are becoming increasingly sophisticated for employers wishing to self-fund their mental health plans. For example, an employer can now negotiate a capitation rate for mental health care, thereby locking in costs at what should be a substantial discount. Employers skeptical or anxious about capitation can request that the managed mental health care company provide an estimate of savings followed by implementation of the plan on a more standard, fee-for-service basis. Along with this understanding, however, should be monthly financial statements tracking the success or failure of the new company's efforts to contain mental health costs. Employers in such situations should extend contracts for no more than one to three years. If the managed mental health care provider fails to live up to promises, this shorter-term arrangement allows the employer to shop around.

As a further guide for purchasers interested in mental health/substance abuse costs, the following information provides a general range of expectation for cost savings by managed care products. The savings noted in Table 5–1 are primarily a function of the efficient use of inpatient care combined with brief outpatient care designed to handle the greater numbers of visits that managed care typically engenders. Inpatient costs generally consume between 65 and 80 percent of costs of an unmanaged plan. With managed care, however, they will consume only 20 to 40 percent. Managed care will typically bring down inpatient days between 15 and 40 days per 1,000. Outpatient visits, on the other

Table 5–1 Expected Mental
Health/Substance Abuse Costs as
a Function of Insurance Product

Insurance Product	Cost of Mental Health/Substance Abuse as a Percentage of Total Premium
Fee-for-service	14 to 26 percent
Employee Assistance Program	14 to 25 percent
Utilization review only	13 to 21 percent
Preferred practitioner organization	8 to 12 percent
Exclusive provider organization (capitated)	4 to 7 percent
Health maintenance organization	3 to 6 percent

hand, will go up from unmanaged to managed care plans (an average of 200 days per 1,000 and 370 days per 1,000, respectively). The average length of mental health inpatient stay in unmanaged plans is 18 to 20 days versus 10 days with managed care. For substance abuse, the figures are 24 and 5 days, respectively. (Of course, the range around these mean data is substantial.)

Due to the substantial savings derived from more efficient outpatient and inpatient care, managed mental health care companies are in a good position to pass along a significant amount of savings to the employers purchasing these services. Along with savings, the employer should also be able to receive additional services, such as those discussed here.

Management information systems (MIS) give companies the capability to report costs back to employers in a variety of ways. Analyses can include total dollars spent on mental health/substance abuse; costs as a percentage of total premium; inpatient costs versus outpatient costs; type of user (employee, dependent, adult, adolescent); age and sex of consumers; days per thousand on an inpatient and outpatient basis; hospital days and average lengths of stay by institutional provider; and a variety of data categorized by the diagnoses of patients requiring mental health treatments.

Managed mental health care companies should be able to provide or disclose an extensive format for credentialing providers and for assuring that providers meet reasonable and appropriate standards. A list of references of the companys' customers should be obtained. Such companies are usually willing to provide answers to rather detailed questions about operations, clinical standards, credentialing, and so forth. These can be obtained in writing, both as a means of monitoring services as well as of understanding how companies of this nature do business.

The company retained should have a reputation for integrity and patient advocacy. In this sense, the purchaser should demand to see what type of quality assurance programs the company has in place. A minimum would include a demonstration of capacity to detect good and bad provider performance, resolve grievances, note early onset of malpractice or incompetence, obtain knowledge of relevant outcome research so that the purchaser's clientele will receive state-of-the art care, establish tracking systems for medications and appropriate psychotherapies by disorder, and maintain feedback loops for both the recognition and correction of mistakes.

Managed care companies putting capitation before service are more likely to deny appropriate care. This can be observed through valid consumer complaints or through other forms of hard data, including the number of readmissions to the hospital within two to four weeks after the initial inpatient discharge and additional requests for outpatient services following formal terminations of care. Reputable firms are willing to track such data and provide them to purchasers as part of contractual arrangements.

Where possible, prospective purchasers should meet the top management, or management representatives, of the managed mental health care company whose services are under bid. It is also very important to meet the medical and executive directors of the local subsidiaries where the plan will be in place.

Some companies have subsidiaries nationwide and are thus in need of a nationwide mental health care carrier. If the carrier does not have a formal subsidiary or operation in some of the needed sites of the company, the bidder should have a track record of establishing such subsidiaries in a timely fashion. Some mental health care firms have met this challenge by establishing an "employer product," staffed 24 hours a day by clinicians who have access to local provider networks and capabilities of assessing crisis situations by telephone. Such companies will typically have the ability to perform on-site or telephonic review of inpatient cases as they occur.

Some of these services are not available in every company; however, most reputable firms with a national presence will be able to provide a majority of these needs. A list and description of several of the national managed mental health care firms is provided in Chapter 10.

Chapter 6

Inpatient Case Management

Inpatient care traditionally has received relatively complete coverage by third-party payers. This was due in part to the belief that restrictive treatment environments were more likely to be utilized only by patients truly in need. A concomitant belief was that inpatient care resulted in better treatment outcomes.

The dose paradox effect in mental health and substance abuse, however, is perhaps no more in evidence than with inpatient care. Research findings cast doubt on the clinical judgment of some professionals (and insurance representatives) who unduly favor hospital care. This research supports the conclusion, iterated in the next two chapters, that the usual and customary approach to treatment sometimes escalates costs and leads to poorer results.

INPATIENT PSYCHIATRIC CARE

The most provocative and well-cited literature on this subject was compiled by Kiesler (1982), who discussed nine experimental studies—and a quasi-experimental one—used to evaluate the effectiveness of inpatient care in relation to less intensive means of approach. The reader is referred to Kiesler's review for an in-depth discussion of each of these studies. Some will be discussed briefly below and in the subsequent chapter on hospital alternatives.

Inpatient treatment attracted critics long before many of the studies discussed by Kiesler were in print. Flomenhaft, Kaplan, and Langsley (1969), for example, argued that inpatient care depersonalized patients, made them less attractive to employers, fostered dependency, and further stigmatized those whose problems in living were already great. Goffman saw mental hospitals as "total institutions," which he defined as places of residence and work "where a large number of like-situated

74

individuals, cut off from the wider society for an appreciable period of time, together led an enclosed, formally administered round of life" (1961, p. xiii). Several sociologists (e.g., Goldstein, 1979) viewed institutionalization as fostering further institutional dependency, loss of vocational abilities and social functioning, and diminishing contact with relatives and significant others. In the Rosenhan (1975) study, eight normal volunteers reported feelings of powerlessness and depersonalization from their hospital care.

Kiesler's review indicates that some of these worries may be justified. Treatment conditions in the 10 studies included a broad range of alternative care. (Inpatient care was utilized as the comparative control.) In 4 of the studies, the experimental condition was partial care. All of these partial care studies excluded patients who were not a serious danger to themselves or others (exclusion rates ranged from 34 to 78 percent). The other 6 studies used alternative care treatments ranging from hostel care to outpatient crisis intervention. Of these 6 studies, 2 did not exclude any patients; the remaining 4 excluded alcoholism/organic brain syndrome (Stein, Test, & Marx, 1975), all but first-admission schizophrenics (Levenson, Lord, Sermas, Thornby, Sullender, & Comstock, 1977; Mosher, Menn, & Matthews, 1975), and all but 18- to 62-year-old nonlethal schizophrenics (Pasamanick, Scarpitti, & Dinitz, 1967). Patients in these alternative conditions would normally have been treated in a hospital setting had not random assignment dictated otherwise. As indicated, they suffered from severe psychopathologies ranging from schizophrenia to severe depression with suicidal intent.

Significant differences were seen in 9 of the 10 studies, all of which fell in favor of the alternative treatment. (The tenth study, which investigated daycare, showed no difference.) The most common finding, noted in each of the studies in which such data were reported, was that alternative care decreased readmission rates to the hospital. Alternative-care patients were more likely to gain employment, spend time in independent settings, develop friendships, and attain better adjustment on psychometric measures of emotional functioning. To quote Kiesler:

> It seems quite clear from these studies that for the vast majority of patients now being assigned to inpatient units in mental institutions, care of at least equal impact could be otherwise provided. There is not an instance in this array of studies in which hospitalization had any positive impact on the average patient which exceeded that of the alternative care investigated in the study. In almost every case, the alternative care had more positive outcomes. There were significant and powerful effects on such life-related variables as employment, school attendance, and the like. There were significant and important effects on the probability of subsequent re-admission: Not only did the patients in the alternative care not undergo the

initial hospitalization, but they were less likely to undergo hospitalization later, as well. There is clear evidence here for the causal sequence in the finding alluded to earlier that the best predictor of hospitalization is prior hospitalization. These data across these ten studies suggest quite clearly that hospitalization of mental patients is self perpetuating. (1982, pp. 357–358)

A more recent review of partial care outcome, generally reflecting Kiesler's view, is available in Parker and Knoll (1990).

INPATIENT SUBSTANCE ABUSE CARE

Miller and Hester (1986) reviewed 26 controlled studies comparing a variety of conditions allowing efficacy estimations on inpatient care. As with Kiesler's review, Miller and Hester found no advantage of inpatient over day treatment in four controlled studies. Nearly all significant differences favored day treatment. McLachlan and Stein (1982), for example, contrasted a 28-day inpatient program with treatment through a day clinic. At one-year followup, no differences were found on alcohol or drug use, emotional adjustment, assertiveness, or marital communication. The day clinic clients incurred 79 percent fewer days of hospitalization during the followup year, compared with their use during the pretreatment year, whereas those treated in the hospital showed a 38 percent increase in subsequent year hospitalization. (This was statistically significant.) There were 75 percent fewer readmissions for day clinic clients and 4 percent fewer among inpatients, also statistically significant.

Longabaugh, McCrady, Fink, Stout, McAuley, Doyle, and McNeill (1983) randomly assigned clients either to a 14-day inpatient program or to 15 weekdays of care in a day hospital. There were no significant differences at 6-month followup. At 24-month followup, the day patients were significantly more improved on measures of abstinence, emotional adjustment, and life satisfaction.

In an interesting study evaluating the effects of staff density, Stinson, Smith, Amidjaya, and Kaplan (1979) randomly assigned 466 alcoholics either to a staff-intensive residential setting or to a peer-oriented program. (This latter treatment program emphasized self-direction.) At 18-month followup, patients in the less intensive program showed significantly greater improvement on drinking behavior. No other significant differences were observed.

Miller and Hester located 10 studies comparing inpatient with outpatient care. Several of these were uninterpretable due to violation of random assignment. In general, there were few significant differences across studies, and nearly all of the significant differences favored outpatient care. Wilson, White, and Lange (1978), for example, compared 45 alcoholics receiving inpatient care with 45 others randomly assigned to outpatient programs in the community. Outpatients showed significantly better self-concept, general adjustment, and reduction in alcoholic symptoms at five-month followup. Smart, Finley, and Funston (1977) reported a 50 percent success rate among outpatients at six-month followup, compared with 25 percent among those treated on an inpatient basis.

In a widely cited study, Orford, Oppenheimer, and Edwards (1976) compared 50 alcoholics receiving inpatient and outpatient treatment with 50 others randomly assigned to evaluation-only followed by one session of outpatient therapy. No significant differences were found between groups on any measure at one- and two-year followups. Quoting Miller and Hester about these studies:

> Although each of these controlled studies of inpatient care can be faulted on specific methodological points, the combined results of all 16 are quite consistent. In no case was residential care found to yield superior improvement relative to less expensive treatment alternatives. To the contrary all observed differences favored nonresidential settings. (1986, p. 799)

Miller and Hester (1986) reported no advantage over extended inpatient stays, typically 30 days, compared to detoxification-only programs of 7 to 10 days. Improvement was correlated with participation in subsequent outpatient care. Consistent with dose paradox, length of outpatient care failed to be a discriminating variable in this review.

The same types of counterintuitive findings relate to studies on outpatient versus inpatient detoxification. Except in cases where medical conditions preclude outpatient detox, results tend to "wash," and no significant differences emerge (Hayashida, Alterman, McClellan, O'Brien, Purtill, Volpicelli, Raphaelson, & Hall, 1989).

INPATIENT TREATMENT
COINCIDENT WITH
MANAGED CARE

The author has been approached by numerous hospital administrators interested in making their programs more compatible with the needs of managed mental health care. They were generally unaware of the studies discussed in the previous sections. Their intent was primarily to find which programs, services, and/or personnel needed to be added to obtain a competitive niche.

Fee-for-service incentives favor add-ons and ancillaries. (Charges for these services can be added to per diems at a profit.) This was one among many factors causing total daily charges for inpatient care to increase. Having generally the opposite incentive, managed mental health care representatives look to hospitals for innovative, cost-effective programs in concert with the themes just presented. For the hospital administrator seeking a competitive edge in an HMO-dominated marketplace, a number of the concepts (based primarily on minimalization) presented here may be helpful.

Managed mental health care companies are typically in search of the lowest, all-inclusive per diem rate. Occupational therapy, recreational therapy, art therapy, and so forth may not be valued nearly as much as concentrated treatment programs in which research-validated techniques are applied by disorder. These latter programs are less cost and staff intensive.

Managed mental health care representatives worry especially about the first 24 to 48 hours subsequent to hospital admission. They note that patients are often easier to get in the hospital than to get out. The greatest number of charges tend to occur at the time of admission. Administrators sensitive to this concern may wish to set aside first-day beds for managed care clientele, which entail program "scale-backs" and which allow thorough evaluation by the managed care attending physician before an inpatient or partial care bed (or transfer) is approved. Bethesda PsychHealth Hospital in Denver established for managed care the Rapid Care Unit for the provision of immediate treatment, stabilization, and subsequent transfer to partial care or outpatient care. Also welcome was Bethesda's prescreening of attending physicians willing to work according to managed care stipulations.

Some psychiatric hospitals specialize in long-term treatment of adolescents, especially those suffering from conduct disorder. Managed mental health care is most unlikely to authorize such treatment. Except in severe cases (e.g., where lethality is involved), managed care will instead insist on outpatient psychotherapy. Juvenile, parental, and other authorities, however, will pressure managed care to provide hospital services to youths who threaten to run away, defy parental management at home, or repeat criminal offenses. This puts the hospital administrator in a position of providing at least a modicum of satisfaction to conflicting parties. Specifically, managed care might welcome as a compromise a hospital unit in which adolescents can be rapidly assessed, provided daily family therapy, and fit into a structured program in which treatment and discharge to outpatient care can be managed in four to six days.

Managed mental health care companies may soon be setting up their own daycare treatment centers (see Chapter 7). Hospital administrators who wish to interface with such systems might consider proffering attractive evening rates for patients still needing the security of an overnight stay.

These recommendations may apply to substance abuse facilities as well. Facility administrators should place emphasis on day care treatment as well as on the establishment of intensive outpatient programs to which managed care can refer. They might also set up treatment modules in line with the research literature. A promising approach is that of Azrin (1976), recommended particularly strongly in the Miller and Hester article discussed earlier.

Miller and Hester (1986) discussed correlational data suggesting that chronic and very severe alcoholics ("gamma" alcoholics) fare better with inpatient rehabilitation. Such data open the door for the utilization of psychometrically sophisticated screening instruments that discriminate such patients from those less impaired. Treatment for gamma alcoholics could then be provided via intensive 7- to 14-day inpatient rehabilitation programs.

Managed mental health care systems significantly curtail psychiatric/substance abuse admissions and lengths of stay such as were observed through much of the 1960s and 1970s. As the grip of managed care tightens further around the market, a greater necessity for innovations (such as those discussed earlier) will be observed.

As indicated, large psychiatric facilities with an abundance of add-on services labor in a business climate antipodean to that which managed mental health care will pursue. Except for cases of grave lethality or mental disability, such facilities, where managed mental health care is strong, become superannuated. The program of the future will be the hospital alternative. Some examples of this coming approach will be provided in the subsequent chapter.

Examples of Managed Inpatient Care

Although managed care tends to rely upon empirical results, the *application* of research-validated concepts (such as variable lengths of stay and treatment in least restrictive settings) can be difficult and complicated. The following case illustrations demonstrate how inpatient treatment is authorized and subsequently used by managed care systems.

CASE ILLUSTRATION 1*

Janet was a 35-year-old, married Caucasian female with one child, age 8. Before switching to an HMO, she had been treated for major depression for five years by a licensed psychologist. During the most acute phase of her illness she suffered suicidal ideation. She denied current intent or plan.

The treatment had originally explored the patient's feelings about her abusive husband. In the last eight months of treatment, however, the patient had begun to uncover past memories of physical and sexual abuse from her father. With the uncovering of these past memories, Janet's depression began to worsen, and she began making superficial cuts on her wrists every few weeks. She began sleeping poorly, losing weight, and feeling so exhausted that her work performance and attendance began to suffer. Her boss was very unhappy about this.

Following an argument about finances, Janet's husband slapped her and demanded a divorce. She took 10 sleeping pills and called an ambulance. After obtaining treatment in the emergency room, Janet denied being suicidal. When her therapist came to see her in the emergency room, she relayed that she could not get memories of the abuse off of her mind.

The psychologist was not a member of the new provider panel for the HMO. The HMO required preauthorization for inpatient admission. The HMO also required that patients obtain services from in-network providers. The psychologist called the director of the HMO to demand two to three weeks of inpatient treatment with hypnotherapy in order to work through her abuse memories in a safe setting. He also demanded that an exception be made in order for him to be able to continue care both on an inpatient and an outpatient basis.

The HMO arranged for an evaluation the next morning. At this point, the patient continued to deny suicidal ideation, plan, or intent, and responded well to a no-suicide contract with the evaluator (also a psychologist). The HMO also arranged for Janet to get a psychiatric evaluation that day. The psychiatrist diagnosed major depressive disorder, recurrent, moderate to severe. With the patient's consent, he prescribed a trial of a tricyclic along with periodic blood work to ensure compliance and proper dosage level.

Janet indicated that she had been reluctant to go into the hospital but, after further discussion with her psychologist, felt that it might be a good idea. She stated that she felt much better because her husband had apologized so profusely after the fight.

---

* Portions of this case were presented at the convention of Communities for a Drug Free Colorado, discussed in Chapter 1 (Giles, 1990c).

The evaluator explained to Janet that her new insurance covered out-patient treatment on a short-term, directive basis only. He supported her initial reluctance to go into the hospital, explaining that the HMO used hospitalization judiciously. He stated that hospitalization would indeed be an option if the patient had recurrent suicidal thoughts and did not improve from the new care. There was a positive family history for depression, and the evaluator explained that medication, combined with a type of attitude change therapy, might help her feel much better. The evaluator said that further treatment with the psychologist would not be covered beyond transition (six visits). He informed the patient of her benefit maximum of twenty outpatient sessions per calendar year.

Further evaluation indicated that the patient did not suffer from an Axis II disorder. The evaluator informed Janet of the risk of one hospitalization leading to another. With patient consent, the evaluator spoke to the EAP director, who had relayed a threat of job loss from absenteeism. This threat was also discussed with Janet during the evaluation. Janet decided to try medication along with cognitive therapy in a group for women. She told her psychologist that she could not continue treatment due to the drain on the family's funds. The psychologist wrote a formal letter of complaint to the HMO.

In addition to the treatment plan described above, the HMO arranged for Janet to receive marital treatment in order to attempt to break the abuse cycle. Because HMO benefits included 15 group visits per calendar year along with 20 individual/family sessions, Janet was able to be seen two or three times per week during the first month after her crisis. The HMO arranged for her to see the psychiatrist on the hour immediately following marital treatment. (This arrangement prevented a benefit session from being utilized for psychiatric consultation.)

Janet responded fairly well to the medication/psychotherapy regimen and did not require hospitalization. Treatment stressed cognitive change, assertiveness training, independence skills, and marital intervention. Although the couple continued to suffer arguments, violence did not erupt again, and the marriage remained intact.

CASE ILLUSTRATION 2

The patient, Jimmy, a 9-year-old boy, was taken to a children's psychiatric facility late on a Sunday evening. The parents stated that Jimmy had pulled a knife on his younger brother and threatened to kill him.

This hospital was one of two facilities under contract with the HMO carrying this family's benefits. Hospital officials were aware that a life-threatening emergency precluded the HMO's necessity for preadmission review. They admitted the boy for inpatient care, sent the parents home, and alerted the HMO to the admission the following morning.

Although under contract, this particular hospital had not been utilized much by the HMO for psychiatric services. The HMO was especially wary of this hospital because of its reputation for long lengths of stay. However, the beds on the children's unit at the HMO's primary hospital were full. The HMO's chief psychiatrist, Dr. Keane, was too busy to take on Jimmy's case; however, she agreed to act as a consultant and concurrent reviewer.

The attending physician on this case, Dr. Jones, was one of the HMO's contractors but was not a wholehearted supporter of managed care. He diagnosed attention deficit disorder and prescribed Ritalin. At a staff meeting on Wednesday, a treatment plan calling for 30 to 40 days of inpatient care was recommended. (Dr. Jones concurred.) Treatment was to consist of milieu, medication management, and play therapy.

The HMO balked at this recommendation and asked Dr. Keane to provide an evaluation and second opinion. The HMO also insisted on family therapy and arranged for a licensed clinical social worker to see Jimmy and his family on a nightly basis.

Both parents refused to cooperate with family therapy and failed to show up for appointments. In lieu of family treatment, the social worker met with Jimmy alone. During the course of the first two visits, Jimmy denied wanting to kill his brother. He said that his knife was made of harmless flexible plastic without a point.

Dr. Keane concurred with the diagnosis of attention deficit disorder as well as with the recommended medication treatment. Dr. Keane did not, however, agree that the boy was violent. Based on her assessment as well as her consultation with the social worker, she recommended to Dr. Jones that the boy be discharged back to his parents' home that evening. Dr. Jones and the hospital staff objected strenuously to the recommendation for discharge. They communicated their displeasure to Jimmy's parents, who subsequently refused to come and get the child.

Jimmy was an adopted child of his father's first marriage. He did not get along with his new stepmother, and she persuaded Jimmy's father to relinquish him back to Social Services. The parents intended to begin relinquishment proceedings and to keep the boy in the hospital while Social Services began working out the details. They stated to Dr. Keane that their policy covered 45 days per calendar year and that they fully intended to use all of it. They continued to refuse to participate in family therapy.

This scenario attracted a great deal of discussion among Dr. Keane and the executive director of the Plan. They subsequently informed the hospital and parents by letter that the insurance covered inpatient psychiatric care to the extent deemed medically necessary. The letter indicated that medical necessity did not include custodial care and that the boy was ready to go home. It went on to state that outpatient family therapy would be authorized by medical/psychiatric representatives of the HMO. These representatives, Dr. Keane in particular, did not believe that relinquishment would be in the best interest of the child.

The letter was unsuccessful in getting either the parents or the hospital to change their respective positions. The HMO responded that reimbursement for hospital charges would not continue beyond the initial assessment and recommendation period. Dr. Keane empathized with the dissenting opinions but indicated that further treatment would be paid for by the hospital itself and not by the HMO. The letter also reminded the hospital administrator of the "hold harmless" clause in the HMO contract: Charges billed to the HMO but denied could not be charged back to the family of the patient.

With some encouragement by hospital staff, the parents threatened to sue Dr. Keane and the HMO. After reviewing the case, the attorney for the HMO indicated that Dr. Keane was on solid ground and should resist this pressure.

Following three additional weeks of unauthorized inpatient care, Jimmy's parents agreed to try the HMO's recommendation for family treatment as a last resort to relinquishment. The hospital staff discharged Jimmy to his parents' home, and family therapy began. The parents also decided not to litigate at that time. The remaining issue was that of the unpaid balance of the bill.

The vice president of operations for the HMO visited this subsidiary one month after Jimmy's discharge. He agreed to meet with the hospital administrator in order to discuss the case further. In the interest of goodwill, the vice president agreed to pay an additional $2,000 of the unpaid balance. In a subsequent letter, he stated that the additional monies were for purposes of continuing the business relationship only and that, in his view, the hospital was guilty of attempting to extend the length of stay beyond medical necessity. He also cited hospital staff for colluding with the parents against the HMO. Further problems of this nature, he wrote, would result in termination of the contract.

CASE ILLUSTRATION 3

Linda was the 16-year-old daughter and only child of a prominent attorney and chief executive officer of a large manufacturing/accounting firm in the South. This gentleman, Mr. Lord, had purchased HMO coverage for himself and his employees, and the HMO had in turn employed a managed mental health care company to handle psychological and psychiatric needs. At the insistence of her parents, Linda went to her doctor for a complete physical and general checkup. At the time of the examination, she weighed 99 pounds and stood 5 feet 4 inches tall. She had refused meals for 10 weeks and had lost 32 pounds. Blood and urine tests were completed, and electrolytes, protein metabolism, and liver, kidney, and cardiac functioning were all found to be normal. Linda's parents, however, reported that she was exhausted, confused, and depressed.

Linda's appetite was strong, although she was proud to be able to resist to it. She was terrified of gaining weight, stating that she "felt fat." Her menstrual periods were irregular. She seemed shy and socially inhibited, had few friends, and spoke monosyllabically to her parents. She was a straight A student in school and trained regularly for the high school cross-country team.

Linda's weight loss precipitated a major crisis in the family. Both parents were extremely worried about her and called her doctor several times to get his advice. The physician indicated that Linda suffered from anorexia nervosa, a severe eating disorder with high mortality. He recommended that Linda be hospitalized for 45 days at the local psychiatric facility.

Upon learning of her parents' intention to place her in the hospital, Linda, who was eating only green vegetables once a day, stated that she would starve herself completely if forced to go to an inpatient ward. She denied any need for treatment, stating that she had never felt better in her life.

At a premorbid weight of 130 pounds, Linda tried out for the cheerleading squad but was not picked. The squad leader indicated that this was because Linda was "too fat," also indicating that Linda would be a beautiful girl if she could only lose some weight. Linda's father was overweight and her mother was obese.

Mr. Lord called the general manager and the medical director of the HMO to demand that his daughter receive intensive psychiatric care immediately. It was Mr. Lord's opinion that all 45 available inpatient days would be necessary to help his daughter. These days corresponded with the end-of-the-calendar year when benefits renewed and 45 additional days became available. The general manager called the executive director of the managed mental health care company and relayed Mr. Lord's request. The general manager stated that the inpatient request was appropriate. Since Mr. Lord's account comprised a major part of the HMO membership, the general manager also requested that this case be given every consideration. The executive director, a clinical psychologist, agreed to provide an immediate evaluation.

The psychiatrist who evaluated Linda diagnosed her as "eating disorder not otherwise specified" (menstruation continued, which ruled out a diagnosis of anorexia nervosa). Linda denied binging or purging and did not appear to have an Axis II disorder. Although Linda complained of depression, the psychiatrist felt that this—along with other symptoms such as bradycardia, confusion, and fatigue—was secondary to the eating disorder. There was one provider in the network with experience in family therapy for eating disorders. The psychiatrist referred Linda and her family for outpatient treatment with this clinician.

Mr. Lord was furious with this recommendation and with the implication that he was involved in any way with Linda's illness. He again insisted on inpatient treatment and called the general manager and the executive director to voice protestations and complaints. Mr. Lord refused to come to therapy until or unless his daughter was hospitalized. Linda, happy not to be forced into the hospital, agreed to see the therapist instead.

The executive director called the vice president and corporate medical director at the parent firm. This company had gotten the HMO's business in a bid against four other competing firms. After six months' experience with this account, it had become evident that the capitation was not high enough to cover subsequent use (which, on an inpatient basis especially, was much higher than expected). This company was losing about $10,000 per month on the account, and the pressure from Mr. Lord and the general manager for 45 to 90 inpatient days was met with alarm. Neither the corporate medical director nor the subsidiary psychiatrist, however, specialized in the treatment of eating disorders.

Linda liked her new therapist, a licensed clinical social worker, and began to talk to her about low self-esteem, problems with her family, and her many sensitivities to rejection. After six weeks of treatment, however, Linda's parents had still refused to participate and Linda had lost another five pounds. This precipitated another round of calls to the executive director from Mr. Lord and the general manager. The patient's doctor also began to demand immediate inpatient care. Linda's blood pressure was low, her hair was brittle, and continued lab work indicated that her body was just beginning to metabolize muscle tissue for energy.

The executive director fielded calls from the corporate office as well. He was well aware that his performance ratings, bonus, and continued employment rested in part on the financial results of his plan. However, he did not want to jeopardize the well-being of a patient by denying appropriate inpatient care. Also having little experience with eating disorders, he decided to visit the local medical library to read journal articles on this disorder.

Once this literature review was complete, the executive director picked three names of well-known experts and eventually located one who was willing to provide consultation and supervision on this case. The executive director, after obtaining appropriate releases of information, sent his clinician's case notes to this consultant (a psychiatrist at a hospital in Massachusetts). A conference call was then arranged between the psychiatrist consultant, the executive director, the general manager, Mr. and Mrs. Lord, and Linda.

Before the conference call, the executive director met with Linda's parents. He apologized for seeming to work against what Linda's parents perceived to be in her best interests. He stated that he was not an expert in eating disorders and so had hired the consultant to help them all reach a proper decision. He also stated that while cost containment was of interest to him and to his firm, a preemptive interest was quality care and patient safety. He was thus hoping that the consultant would be able to recommend the most appropriate direction in which to proceed.

The consultant began the conference with notice that she was a "free agent," unencumbered by obligations to the insurance company or to the parents that might bias her judgment unduly. She explained her credentials and arranged to send along reprints of research she had published on treatment of eating disorders.

She empathized with the parents' concern, saying that anorexia is associated with high mortality (5 percent) and only about a 35 percent complete improvement rate. In addition to mortality, the psychiatrist reported that about a third of anorexics "float" in and out of hospitals for the rest of their lives. With this, she praised the executive director for attempting to treat this case on an outpatient basis.

The psychiatrist indicated that hospitalization for anorexia is by no means a panacea and is sometimes associated with clinical deterioration, especially with lengths of stay less than six to eight months. She explained that hospitalization risked increasing Linda's anger and sense of loss of control, making her in turn more likely to become dependent on inpatient care. She said that she was assured of the executive director's willingness to hospitalize if necessary, indicating that this would indeed be unfortunate given that relatively brief hospitalizations for anorexia should be utilized as a last resort. The recommendation, if at all possible, was for intensive outpatient care.

The psychiatrist admonished the parents for failing to cooperate with treatment and urged them to participate in family therapy on a twice-a-week basis. She also urged them, for their daughter's sake, to accept that they might be playing, albeit inadvertently, some role in their daughter's problem. She indicated that anorexic families tended to be overconcerned about each other's private affairs and tended toward communication patterns that failed to foster the identified patient's self-esteem.

The psychiatrist went on to recommend the type of inpatient program that would need to be set up if Linda continued to deteriorate. She emphasized, and fully detailed, a contingency management program to induce anorexics to gain weight on an inpatient basis. She said that hyperalimentation should be avoided if possible in favor of requiring Linda to gain and maintain her weight by ingesting a broad array of both low-calorie and high-calorie foods.

She encouraged the family with the availability of good prognostic signs: Linda's relatively young age of onset, her lack of purgative use, and the relative lack of overtly aggressive or hostile communications between family members. On the other hand, the family was cautioned not to expect immediate or great improvement. The psychiatrist said that they should count their blessings if Ms. Anderson, the licensed clinical social worker, could help Linda stay well enough to avoid hospitalization. She urged Linda to stop denying the severity of her illness, to cooperate fully with Ms. Anderson, and to attempt wherever possible to face her fears of food by expanding her menu as much as possible.

The psychiatrist went on to detail her preference, should more restrictive treatment be necessary, for partial care for this problem. She recommended contingency management to induce three meals per day followed by a discharge home each evening. The rationale, again, was that a partial program might undercut the dependency and rehospitalization that could ensue from full inpatient care.

The family subsequently participated in outpatient care. Also, under the consultant's supervision, Ms. Anderson began to apply cognitive and desensitization techniques for Linda's body image distortion (see Chapter 8). Additional emphasis was placed on Linda's feelings of worthlessness and devastation from criticism. As these feelings emerged, Linda began distracting herself less with thoughts of starvation. Finally, with the help of a nutritionist, Ms. Anderson helped Linda experiment with types and amounts of food, eaten at first with a companion and later alone, which, though still characterizing an anorexic eating style, maintained health and weight status enough to avoid emergency hospital care.

After a year of treatment, Linda showed stable medical signs and maintained a weight of 94 pounds. The year was difficult for her and her parents. Linda suffered two relapses, requiring brief partial care stays at the local psychiatric facility. Family therapy was successful in removing Linda from a mediational role, but this in turn led to increased marital conflict and a brief separation. With improved nutrition, Linda's depression, confusion, and dizziness remitted.

At a two-year followup, Linda weighed 103 pounds and was doing well in her college freshman courses.

CASE ILLUSTRATION 4

Gaylen was brought to a psychiatric emergency room by the police after threatening to shoot his lover in a bar. He was covered under an HMO insurance plan that capitated mental health services to a local provider group. Upon notice of admission, the utilization review nurse went to the psychiatric emergency room to complete an evaluation. The detaining officer indicated that Gaylen had been drinking heavily and that his behavior seemed out of control, impulsive, and bizarre. Once the interview began, Gaylen informed the R.N. that he had serious problems with drugs and alcohol. Gaylen consumed half a gallon of Jack Daniels per week, mainly on the weekend. He smoked two to four "little rocks" of crack cocaine on a daily basis. He denied current usage of other illicit drugs.

He was oriented to time, place, and person, and was cooperative with the interviewer. He denied any recent head injury or other trauma. He also denied significant medical history (seizures, cardiological problems, gastrointestinal disease, liver dysfunction) and stated that he had "hit bottom" and had realized that he desperately needed help.

Gaylen's history of drug use began with "social drinking and running with the wrong crowd" in college 10 years earlier. This led to experimentation with marijuana, cocaine, and crack. Crack use had been ongoing for six months. Gaylen had held a job in good standing for the last two years at a local convenience store. He did not wish to miss work and asked that his problems be held in confidence from his employer.

This patient had recently broken up from a relationship with a gay lover and was severely distraught. He denied suicidal ideation, plan, intent, or history but admitted to feelings of rage toward his lover. He stated that the gun was unloaded (this subsequently was proven true) and that its use was to provide no harm other than a good scare. Before the incident, Gaylen had attempted to stop using crack. His last prior use had been three weeks before the incident.

In the prior two years, Gaylen had withdrawn from crack or alcohol "cold turkey" on two occasions and had remained abstinent for periods of two weeks and two months, respectively. This "abstinence," however, was from one drug or the other. Gaylen had been unable to quit use of both alcohol and crack at the same time. He denied any significant withdrawal symptoms other than a one- or two-day hangover consisting of nausea and headache.

Following this interview, the nurse contacted the firm's addictionologist to consult about the possibility of outpatient detoxification. The clinical director for the firm's outpatient chemical dependency treatment program was also consulted. They decided not to attempt outpatient detoxification. Other than his former lover, who was no longer around, Gaylen had no close friends or relatives who could sit with him and monitor his well-being on a daily basis. Also, there was no past experience with withdrawal from crack and alcohol at the same time.

Gaylen was referred for social setting detoxification at a freestanding chemical dependency treatment center. His vital signs were monitored daily by the staff physician. He passed through the "euthymic" phase of crack withdrawal, a period characterized by freedom from drug craving. The posteuthymic stage is characterized by hyperemotionality, extreme frustration and craving, and increased predisposition toward violent behavior (Stalcup, 1989). The staff physician prescribed medication to help Gaylen with his physical cravings. To help extinguish conditioned cravings, Gaylen was placed in a cocaine/crack treatment group at the treatment facility and, in addition to standard counseling interventions, was shown with the group a video of scenes involving common crack or cocaine paraphernalia and situations of use. All of the group members reported strong cravings induced by the video scenes but, due to the inpatient setting, were able to resist. As the video was played repeatedly, cravings diminished greatly.

After nine days on the unit, Gaylen was released to an outpatient chemical dependency program structured by the managed mental health care firm. He was seen twice weekly in group and asked to attend two or three additional Alcoholics Anonymous meetings each week (verified by his sponsor). His lack of relatives living nearby precluded participation in the weekly family therapy program, but Gaylen requested individual treatment to help him adjust better to his homosexuality. The group and individual sessions also uncovered tendencies toward significant social fear and depression. Both of these issues were included in the ongoing treatment plan.

Gaylen was slowly transitioned to the firm's aftercare program, based closely upon Azrin's (1976) model. This included disulfram, structured group support, structured social activities incompatible with drinking, vocational counseling and job support, and weekly group meetings at the clinic. Relapse prevention training was also included posttreatment. According to data collected at an 18-month followup, these interventions had a fairly significant and positive impact on Gaylen's life. He had suffered two relapses, recovering from both on an outpatient basis. At time of followup, he was drug and alcohol free.

Chapter 7
Hospital Alternatives

As indicated in Chapter 6, some inpatient care tends to be inefficient. Some of this is due to the treatment modality (milieu) that hospitals generally employ. The milieu is a therapeutic environment that is standardized across patients. Patients are expected to adjust from their own environments to that of the hospital's. Once adjustment is made, the patient is then expected to adjust back to the environment that was initially problematic. There is no guarantee that a good response to the inpatient setting will generalize home. These inherent problems and possible inefficiencies pave the way for alternatives to hospital care (Kiesler, 1982; Miller & Hester, 1986; also see Braun, Kochansky, Shapiro, Greenberg, Gudeman, Johnson, & Shore, 1981; Parker & Knoll, 1990).

Managed mental health care companies have long been aware of the cost and treatment advantages of daycare. They have not yet begun to set up their own daycare centers, but this step may be observed in the near future. There are several interesting and provocative examples of problem-focused treatments, on both an outpatient and a residential basis, that hold promise for future efforts to contain inpatient costs and to increase the quality of care.

OUTPATIENT ALTERNATIVES

Pasamanick, Scarpitti, and Dinitz (1967) completed a controlled trial with schizophrenic patients, comparing (1) a medication group *remaining at home* who received neuroleptics along with psychiatric care and frequent home visits by a public health nurse; (2) a placebo group treated identically except for the substitution of a placebo for active medication; and (3) a hospital control group admitted for standard hospital treatment. Some 152 admittable schizophrenic patients were randomly assigned to these conditions. Of the total, 90 percent were followed for 6 to 30 months posttreatment (also see the five-year followup in Davis, Dinitz, & Pasamanick, 1972).

Outcomes were significantly better for the home patients treated with active medications. Hospital patients suffered the highest readmission rates (46 percent of hospital control patients versus 24 percent of the home-medicated patients). Improvement in psychiatric symptomatology was found in all groups across most of the instruments used. Similar results were obtained in ratings by significant others.

Study strengths included random assignment; use of highly disturbed, admittable patients; multiple outcome measures, including "hard" data (such as rates of readmission); a large sample size; long-term followup; and high coverage rates at followup. Several methodological problems existed however.

The researchers did not adequately describe the composition of the hospital treatment. Ratings were not blind, and there was no reported information on possible differences between subjects with regard to drug histories, drug effects, drug dosages, and adequacy of medication compliance. Exclusion criteria and geographical restrictions reduced by 69 percent the total pool of referred patients. Exclusions included patients without families and patients who were homicidal, suicidal, or outside of the 18- to 60-year-old admission range. These exclusions limit the degree to which these findings can be generalized to managed care settings.

Langsley, Flomenhaft, and Machotka (1969) assigned 300 patients either to family crisis therapy (FCT) or to hospital care. Other than requiring an ongoing family environment, there were apparently no exclusion criteria for the outpatient subjects despite a high incidence of actively psychotic and suicidal patients. Baseline measures were taken of social adaptation, general functioning, and crisis management. The randomization was apparently successful since no significant differences emerged between groups on pretreatment assessments.

Patients admitted to the hospital were treated with group and individual psychotherapy, milieu, medications, and ancillary treatments. Their average length of stay was 28.6 days. Treatment of the FCT cases was provided by a clinical team on a 24-hour a day, 7-day per week basis. It consisted of an average of 4.2 office visits per patient, 1.3 home visits, 5.4 telephone calls, and 1.2 collateral contacts with social agencies. Length of this treatment averaged 24.2 days.

All 150 FCT cases were treated without admission to the hospital. At 6-month followup, 29 percent of the hospital cases had been readmitted, compared to a 13 percent admission rate for FCT cases. Lengths of stay for the hospital group were nearly three times as long as for the FCT group. FCT patients lost an average of 5 days from normal functioning during treatment, compared with 23 days for the inpatient group. The

FCT group also showed better (more independent) functioning group during the followup period. Psychiatric measures showed general improvement across conditions, but no significant differences emerged. Cost analyses indicated that the FCT treatment cost 83 percent less than the hospital treatment.

This study also suffered from methodological deficiencies. These included lack of validity/reliability estimates on the psychometric outcome measures; lack of detail as to age, range, or severity of specific diagnoses; lack of standardization for the drug treatment regimen across conditions; lack of explanation as to medication management per se; use of assessors who were not blind to conditions; and few ratings of outcome or satisfaction by the patients themselves.

Despite these shortcomings, the results are suggestive. The problems with the psychometric measures, for example, are mitigated by the fact that the hard data (e.g., readmission rates) favored outpatient care. Although poorly described, the hospital treatment seemed comprehensive and comparative in quality to many good inpatient programs. The indication that such a small dose of outpatient care could compare favorably to hospitalization is a result badly in need of replication and extension.

Polak and Kirby (1976) randomly assigned 85 adults of varying diagnoses, all of whom normally would have received hospitalization, either to inpatient treatment or to "total community care." The community care included six small, community-based therapeutic environments (often homes of volunteers), crisis intervention, home treatment, social systems intervention, and rapid tranquilization. Outcome measures were taken across therapists, significant others, and patients themselves (reliability data also provided). The diagnositic range, including percentage of patients per diagnostic category, was reported, and therapists did not vary by condition. There was a 4-month followup which recovered more than 80 percent of the patients.

An unfortunate limitation to this study was the necessity to drop 10 patients from the outpatient group because their symptoms deteriorated beyond levels sustainable with the home care condition. When these 10 patients were excluded from statistical analyses, significant-other ratings for treatment outcome satisfaction showed a difference in favor of the home group. Client ratings also favored the home group on outcome satisfaction, general treatment effectiveness, and perceived staff concern and competence. The researchers reported an inpatient rate of less than 3 days per 1,000 for the home group. (With subsequent experience, this rate reduced to less than 1 day per 1,000.)

These data are impressive enough to suggest that managed mental health care companies will eventually experiment with such models.

This approach is ripe for the entrepreneur willing to set up and sell such services to managed care. If such experimentation proves successful, then quality of care and cost might improve simultaneously. Interested parties should make sure to evaluate outcomes thoroughly and objectively.

RESIDENTIAL ALTERNATIVES

Although an emphasis on outpatient alternatives to inpatient care may be expected from managed care in coming years, there also appears to be room for cost and clinical modifications to traditional inpatient programs. Available empirical work appears to support this change.

Brook (1973) completed a naturalistic, quasi-experimental study precipitated by the temporary closure of the inpatient unit at the Fort Logan Mental Health Center in Denver, Colorado. During the closure period, patients who ordinarily would have been hospitalized were instead placed in a "hostel." These 49 hostel residents were compared with the previous 49 patients admitted to the Fort Logan inpatient unit. Nearly half of the hostel patients were considered to be of moderate to high suicide risk. Half were schizophrenic (half of these chronic), one-fourth were depressive-reactive, and the remaining quarter suffered from various problems including alcohol or drug abuse/dependency, severe adjustment reactions, and so forth. Of these 49 patients, 11 cases had had prior hospitalization.

The hostel had no residential staffing. Neighbors and volunteers helped with meals. Individual and family treatment were conducted both at the hostel and at home. Mean length of stay was 5.75 days.

There were no differences between groups on any of the 11 outcome measures immediately posttreatment. The hostel group, however, suffered fewer remissions of symptoms at followup. (Medication management was not standardized across groups. The hostel group received significantly more medication.) Six of the hospital patients were subsequently readmitted within six months. Three of them were admitted twice. Only one of the hostel patients was readmitted to inpatient care within six months after discharge.

Stein, Test, and Marx (1975) randomly assigned patients either to a community living model or to regular inpatient care. Only patients with organic brain syndrome or primary alcoholism were excluded. All patients had previously spent an average of 14 months in other institutions. The community living approach lasted 14 months, the inpatient care an average of 17 days. At a 4-month followup, there were no differences between conditions in the amount of time spent in nonpsychiatric institutions. There were few differences on other outcome measures;

however, readmission rates were lower for the community treatment. Patients treated in this condition were significantly more likely to spend time in independent settings and to be employed. The community program was also more cost effective than inpatient care.

The results of this study were essentially replicated by Mosher, Menn, and Matthews (1975), who compared the outcome of first-admission schizophrenics randomly assigned either to usual inpatient care or to a residential, home-like facility. At discharge, residential patients had better scores on measures of emotional adjustment. They were more likely to be employed and to be living in independent settings. At a 2-year followup (Matthews, Roper, Mosher, & Menn, 1979), the patients given usual inpatient care had 20 percent more relapses. Critical assessment of the methodological weaknesses of these studies is available in Braun and colleagues' (1981) review.

Gudeman, Dickey, Evans, and Shore (1985) reported results of the rearrangement of their inpatient unit so that all patients were subsequently admitted to the day hospital first. Day hospital treatment included group and family therapy, medication, occupational therapy, vocational counseling, and recreational counseling. Patients requiring overnight stays were usually accommodated at an "inn," open between 4:00 P.M. and 8:00 A.M. weekdays, 24 hours a day on weekends. (Very seriously ill patients were transferred to an intensive care, inpatient unit.) The researchers reported results of the first two years' experience with the new program compared to the two years immediately preceding its development.

Although the hospital's average daily census remained the same, the proportion of day hospital patients increased from 19 to 72 percent. There was a significant decrease in the proportion of patients receiving inpatient and overnight care. The average length of stay decreased in the new program by 20 percent. Readmission rates stayed the same, as did the number of security and medical emergencies. There was a 17 percent decrease in the number of staff accidents and injuries, and patient escapes reduced by 64 percent. Rates of seclusion showed a similar decline. Additionally, the new program allowed a 15.6 percent decrease in direct care staff. The new program decreased costs by 14 percent.

In Denver, a branch of the psychiatric facility for the Colorado Health Sciences Center has been set aside at the Davis Pavilion as an inpatient alternative for managed care patients. This program took the unusual (and appreciated) step of requesting the design opinions of several managed care representatives before the program was fully developed. Many ancillary services have been deleted from this program, but greater emphasis has been placed on directive treatment and crisis intervention.

Patients too ill for this open unit are first hospitalized in a full inpatient bed. Questionable patients are placed on observation for 24 hours at the alternative bed rate. Daycare is given emphasis at this program: morning, afternoon, and evening/overnight care units (or their combination) are available. Also, 24-hour care on the alternative unit is available. Only those psychiatrists with managed care compatibility are eligible for privileges.

Preliminary data (Neil Baker, 1991, personal communication) indicate that outcome for the Alternatives program is comparable to that of matched controls treated at full inpatient facilities. Lengths of stay are much reduced, and cost savings are about 25%.

The Community Care program in Denver also consulted with managed care representatives in Denver before adding acute care beds to its residential facility. Day programs and overnights are available with this program, as are treatment modules designed for immediate stabilization and crisis intervention. This program has proved applicable for all but acutely lethal individuals or those who are quite mentally disabled. Preliminary outcome data compare with those from inpatient units. Cost savings, however, are 30 to 35 percent.

Although the various studies discussed have been completed with adult patients, similar concepts may well be applicable both to adolescents and to the chemically dependent.

Managed mental health care companies are also using outpatient detoxification programs more frequently. From the studies discussed in the Miller and Hester (1986) review, one can see little advantage in the use of full care (versus day) facilities for all but the most seriously debilitated patients.

Chapter 8

Outpatient Case Management

Outpatient case management is in many ways the essence of managed mental health care. It provides a guide to the general functioning of the new systems of health care control.

As with medicine, it seems odd for corporate executives to be involved in strategic planning for psychotherapeutic intervention. Many executives are not clinically trained and feel out of place where matters of mental health are concerned. These controllers, however, are motivated by a fiscal need for clinical efficiency and efficacy, and they are obtaining advice on this subject from experts knowledgeable of the outcome literature.

Although still representing a minority view, a growing number of professionals believe that research should guide clinical practice. Research has indicated that some treatments yield superior outcome to others, especially for certain disorders. In general, comparatively superior treatments are goal directed and time sensitive.

HISTORICAL ROOTS

Although there are relatively few classical psychoanalysts practicing today, a number of concepts from the original theory underlie the interventions of many currently practicing psychotherapists. For example, Freud did not believe in the value of research based on randomized, clinical samples replete with various safeguards for experimental control. He believed in the *secondary* importance of symptoms: Presenting problems such as anxiety neuroses, obsessions, paranoia, and depression were believed to be the consequence of a conflict between intrapsychic forces. Since he considered the symptom to be the best, albeit unconscious, resolution to this conflict, Freud approached problems via indirect means. By various techniques such as dream analysis, free association, and interpretation of transference, Freud attempted to help his patients become aware of their unconscious distortions. When this insight was gained, and only then, a true cure of the illness was considered to have occurred.

Insight-oriented psychotherapies were extremely popular among U.S. therapists in the mid-twentieth century, and such practitioners quickly dominated the clinical scene. They were not, however, without critics. In the 1950s, several researchers began to subject Freudian assumptions to empirical tests. This was the beginning of the volatile split between the empiricists and the intuitionists—a turbulence that still festers vigorously today.

The first cracks in the egg appeared with the publication of a review of studies by H. J. Eysenck, professor at the Maudsley Hospital in London, indicating that the majority of neurotic cases improved within study periods without receipt of therapeutic intervention. This finding was labeled "spontaneous recovery" or "spontaneous remission." The rub occurred when the effects of analytically oriented psychotherapy failed to exceed those observed through spontaneous remission alone. In all but one of the initial studies, effects of treatment failed to exceed those of no treatment. The one study that evidenced superiority of psychotherapy to no treatment showed equivalence to a control group receiving several administrations of an inert pill (see Rachman & Wilson, 1980).

Although fraught with controversy (critics noted that the studies had many methodological deficiencies), these initial challenges formalized several empirical questions about the effectiveness of psychotherapy: (1) Is it more effective than no treatment? (2) Is it more effective than placebo? and (3) Is it more effective than briefer, more directive interventions?

This period also saw the initiation of clinical trials studying the effectiveness of insight-oriented psychotherapy on an open-ended versus a time-limited basis. These studies provided initial demonstration of the dose paradox effect: Additional psychotherapy did not typically lead to better outcome (Rachman & Wilson, 1980).

In the same genre of studies was a group of trials comparing the outcome of paraprofessionals (naturally empathetic individuals without formal clinical training) with the outcome obtained by professional therapists with many years' experience. In the majority of the studies, no differences were obtained (e.g. Zilbergeld, 1983). In more recent studies with tighter methodology (e.g., Strupp & Hadley, 1979), the same result pertained.

Another important impetus behind the scientist/practitioner split was the work of Joseph Wolpe, M.D., a South African psychiatrist. His initial laboratory studies indicated that typical neurotic reactions (such as observed in many depressive and anxiety states) came not as a result of intrapsychic, unconscious forces but through learning processes for which certain organisms, including human beings, appeared particularly adept.

This sort of theorizing led to more directive means of therapeutic change. In addition to a therapeutic technique known as systematic desensitization, Wolpe (1958) advocated present-oriented, educational means of treatment for rapid symptomatic relief (e.g., assertiveness and social skills training, and cognitive restructuring). Finding these new methods more amenable to experimental trial, academicians began subjecting them to empirical tests.

An initial review (Paul, 1969) reported that desensitization was more effective than no treatment, placebo, and insight treatment for anxiety disorders. In a study with surprising methodological sophistication, given the period of its publication, Paul (1966) randomly divided social phobics (whose primary symptom was severe anxiety about speaking in public) into two groups. One group was treated by insight psychotherapy and the other group by desensitization. In order to bypass the problem of therapist bias, Paul trained the analytic therapists to apply desensitization techniques. Both immediately posttreatment and at one-year followup, subjects receiving desensitization showed notably superior results (Paul, 1966; 1967). Successfully treated patients tended to note an amelioration of other symptoms as well.

Given the zeitgeist of the era, such results made the scientist/practitioner split more bitter and irreconcilable (e.g., Glover, 1959). Behavior therapists such as Wolpe and Eysenck did not comprise the only dissenting school. A great deal of subsequent research began to be published on outcomes of cognitive-behavioral and cognitive techniques (e.g., Beck, Rush, Shaw, & Emery, 1979; Beck, 1991). Also making their views heard were family/systems theorists (Minuchin, Rosman, & Baker, 1978), strategic interventionists (Haley, 1963), and a number of other theorists such as Milton Erickson (e.g., Haley, 1973) and David de Shazer (1985). Like behaviorists, these clinicians favored directive, present-oriented interventions for the purpose of arriving at quick solutions to identifiable treatment goals. These latter styles of therapy were also amenable to empirical evaluation (e.g., Minuchin, Rosman, & Baker, 1978).

A number of promising, psychodynamically oriented treatments are also goal-directed and brief-therapy focused. These may well meet the criteria (described later) for inclusion as directive/prescriptive techniques (e.g., Luborsky, 1984; Strupp & Binder, 1984). Therapists interested in an interface with managed mental health care might consider gaining expertise in one or more of these types of intervention.

Traditional treatments typically persist for long periods (months or years), address symptoms indirectly, target general personality change, orient predominantly to childhood events, and prescribe interventions that are primarily interpretive, cathartic, reflective, nondirective, confrontive, and/or transferential (Giles, 1983b).

Directive or prescriptive treatments, on the other hand, are goal and present oriented, behaviorally specific, symptom directive, guided by empirical findings, advice giving, educational, collaborative, and aimed toward the resolution or amelioration of symptoms in relatively brief periods of time (typically 1 to 20 hours of outpatient visits). Several studies (e.g., Sloane, Staples, Cristol, Yorkston, & Whipple, 1975) have indicated that these two types of treatments can be distinguished by blind reviewers listening to taped therapy sessions.

Managed mental health care is theoretically neutral. No specific orientation is preferred *a priori* by training, intuitive preference, or prejudice. The managed care executive is interested primarily in results. In this context, results are determined according to the complex nature of therapeutic outcome itself. In other words, managed mental health care decision makers will demand that treatments, as closely as possible, be chosen and administered according to the best mix of demonstrable results for immediacy of improvement as well as its maintenance, stability, breadth (spread of effect), efficiency, and compatibility with consumer interest and satisfaction.

Managed mental health care, for all its conflicts and difficulties, may represent the single most powerful impetus to the widespread implementation of scientifically validated techniques (Giles, 1990b). The genesis of this change is linked to the new equality between those who pay for services and those who deliver them. Since capitated margins are usually slim, managed systems cannot afford to ignore advances in treatment. These advances are more likely to be passed on from managed care therapists to their patients because immediate psychological improvement correlates with positive fiscal result.

The majority of interventions distinguishing themselves in comparative outcome studies have been behavioral or cognitive-behavioral in nature. In addition to the scientific basis of these therapies, their association with psychotherapy detractors such as H. J. Eysenck and Joseph Wolpe has contributed to many therapists' reluctance to engage in the practice of the new techniques. Such therapists can find excellent treatment models, generally acceptable to managed care, in dynamic, systems, and eclectic theories such as referenced above. It is very important, however, that therapists advertising themselves to be fluent in brief techniques actually have sufficient knowledge and proficiency in this practice. A common complaint from managed care quarters is with reference to therapists who talk in one tongue and practice in another. Such therapists are eventually weeded out of managed care systems in favor of those who are more proficient at brief intervention.

Despite a number of shortcomings in the knowledge base surrounding psychotherapeutic interventions, behavioral and cognitive-behavioral psychotherapies have shown the greatest promise to date in comparative evaluations. Therapists amenable to these new approaches, due to the following advantages, obtain a marketing edge over their traditionally oriented colleagues:

1. Behavioral-cognitive therapies are currently the predominant systems of intervention having different sets of directives specifically applicable by diagnostic category. Thus the "cognitive-behavioral" interventions most effective with panic disorder have little similarity to those developed for the treatment of conduct disorder.
2. They have been shown to enhance therapeutic outcome over no treatment controls, placebo controls, and traditional interventions.
3. They have been shown to be compatible with what the consumer most typically wants from psychological intervention (see below).
4. They are constantly evaluated, updated, and improved by ongoing research conducted in centers all over the world.
5. They are often adaptable to groups.
6. They can be "sold" to managed care on the strength of empirical indications on outcome parameters. For example, with reference to the treatment of bulimia nervosa, treatments emphasizing exposure with response prevention yield significant improvement and/or remission rates of 60 to 70 percent; moderate improvement rates of an additional 15 percent; good evidence of spread of effect, resistance to relapse, and stability; and treatment efficiency averaging 12 to 18 outpatient visits per treatment course. Armed with such data, the therapist-entrepreneur attempting to gain referrals from managed care for difficult and perplexing management problems (such as with bulimics) can garner an interested ear from those charged with the authorization and payment of mental health care.

The following information comprises a brief review of both the consumer preference literature as well as the literature indicating which types of treatment intervention, across several psychological disorders, seem to result in comparative superiority in results. This is not a complete review but is instead an indication for practitioners of a treatment direction that is compatible with, and marketable to, managed mental health care needs.

Consumer Preference

A somewhat surprising literature indicates that the majority of consumers prefer brief psychotherapeutic intervention; for example, 50 percent self-terminate treatment before the fifth visit. This result has been found across community mental health center and private practice populations (Pekarik, 1989). The majority of treatment gain across client populations is obtained by the eighth visit (Pekarik, 1986). The modal number of outpatient visits is one (Pekarik, 1989).

The majority of consumers indicate that they come to treatment not for personality reorganization but for direct advice, brief intervention, and support. This is contrary to the training of many psychotherapists. There are similar findings with regard to reasons why dissatisfied clients drop out. (A significant percentage state that their wishes for brief intervention were incompatible with clinician interests.) Interestingly, a good number of patients expect, and feel satisfied by, only a moderate (as opposed to a very significant or complete) change in their presenting problems. This expectation also tends to cause problems for therapists. For a more complete review of the literature, see Pekarik (1992).

Empirical Support for Prescriptive Therapy

A number of reviewers have concluded that all treatments yield essentially equivalent results (e.g., Luborsky, Singer, & Luborsky, 1975; Smith & Glass, 1977; Stiles, Shapiro, & Elliott, 1986). This indicates that short-term treatments, such as those recommended later in this chapter, do as least as well as the long-term, insight-oriented means of approach. If one goes by these evaluations alone, then prescriptive treatments, being shorter, are more effective. Efficiency is one of a complexity of important factors in the determination of therapy outcome.

Many reviewers of the general outcome literature have themselves been traditionally oriented. Critics (Giles, 1983a, 1983b; Wilson & Rachman, 1983) have reported that significant portions of the outcome literature have been ignored by such reviewers. When the entirety of the literature is considered, a picture different from equivalence seems to emerge.

The bulk of research indicates that general psychotherapy is superior to no treatment. This finding led in part to the proposal that all treatments are equal and work through common, as yet undelineated, mechanisms. Since all therapies presumably include such mechanisms, this hypothesis explains the alleged equivalence of treatments as well as the equivalence between paraprofessionals and experienced psychotherapists.

Therapeutic effects from attention-placebo (or nonspecific) effects should not be disdained. This factor has helped a great number of people suffering from psychological distress (e.g., Andrews & Harvey, 1981; Smith & Glass, 1977; Strupp & Hadley, 1979). This also indicates, however, that clinicians should utilize interventions yielding treatment effects superior to those of nonspecific mechanisms alone.

The equivalists' reviews have as yet failed to include studies from the literature on single-subjects designs, performed to date almost exclusively with prescriptive techniques. For example, a multiple baseline design published by the author and colleagues (Giles, Young, & Young, 1985), discussed further in the section on bulimia nervosa, applied exposure with response prevention techniques, following randomized therapist-attention periods, to 34 severely bulimic subjects. Significant improvement was observed among approximately 70 percent of the sample, and clinical progress occurred in the majority of cases coincident with the onset of the treatment. Those patients unable to comply with treatment recommendations failed to improve. In addition to providing partial validation for previous (and subsequent) reports indicating that such treatment is useful with bulimia, this design allowed an interpretation that the treatment per se, as opposed solely to attentional variables, influenced results. The demonstration of specific treatment effects imputes a possibility of comparative efficacy because such effects have yet to be demonstrated among studies of traditional psychotherapy.

Single-subject methodologies have shown specific effects for such disorders as unipolar depression (e.g., Eisler & Hersen, 1973), marital discord (e.g., Bornstein, 1981; Jacobson, 1977), bulimia nervosa (e.g., Giles, Young, & Young, 1985; Rosen & Leitenberg, 1982), sexual deviations (e.g., Barlow, Leitenberg, & Agras, 1969; Marks & Gelder, 1967), panic disorder (e.g., Ascher, 1981), obsessive-compulsive disorder (e.g., Mills, Agras, Barlow, & Mills, 1973), insomnia (e.g. Turner & Ascher, 1979), sexual dysfunction (e.g., Herman, Barlow, & Agras, 1974), simple phobia (e.g., Lieberman & Smith, 1972), and alcoholism (e.g., Miller, Hersen, Eisler, & Watts, 1974). A more complete review of the use of multiple single-subject designs in relation to comparative outcome may be found in Giles (1993).

There is also evidence that certain types of prescriptive treatments yield outcome superior to attention-placebo for disorders such as primary insomnia (e.g., Ascher & Turner, 1980), marital discord (e.g., Jacobson, 1978), sexual dysfunction (e.g., Marks, 1978), obsessive-compulsive disorder (e.g., Foa, Steketee, & Milby, 1980; Marks, 1982), unipolar depression (e.g., DeRubeis & Hollon, 1981; McLean & Hakstian, 1979), stuttering (e.g., Azrin, Nunn, & Frantz, 1979), tics (e.g., Azrin, Nunn, & Frantz, 1980), problem drinking (e.g., Azrin, 1976; Miller, 1982), simple phobia (e.g., Biran & Wilson, 1980; Gillan & Rachman, 1974), social phobia (Paul, 1966), autism (e.g., Rimland, 1977), panic disorder (e.g., Foa, Jameson, Turner, & Payne, 1980), and bulimia nervosa (Leitenberg, 1992).

The studies cited above compared active treatments either with placebo controls, with alternate directive treatments, or with various combinations of treatment packages. They imply a superiority of directive intervention since the results of more traditional therapies do not usually exceed those of attention controls. For a more complete review of this literature, see Giles (1993).

A number of meta-analytic studies have also provided evidence for the comparative superiority of prescriptive techniques. Smith and Glass (1977), in the original meta-analysis, indicated that systematic desensitization was the most effective therapy. Andrews and Harvey (1981), meta-analyzing psychoneurotic cases, found that general psychotherapy was more effective than no treatment and that directive interventions (typically behavioral therapies) were more effective than general psychotherapy. Two meta-analytic reviews across childhood and adolescent disorders (Casey & Berman, 1985; Weisz, Weiss, Alicke, & Klotz, 1987) also found in favor of directive (usually behavioral) techniques. To quote Weisz and associates, "Behavioral treatments proved superior to non-behavioral treatments regardless of client age, therapist experience, or treated problem" (1987, p. 542).

Much has been made of meta-analytic findings documenting the superiority of general psychotherapy to that of no treatment controls. A reanalysis by Searles (1985) reported that the majority of studies in these reviews evaluated prescriptive and not traditional psychotherapeutic techniques. To quote Searles, "When quality of study is associated with a meta-analysis, the large effect sizes obtained are almost exclusively a function of the positive outcomes of behaviorally-oriented approaches" (1985, p. 460).

There is also a substantial literature in which brief, prescriptive treatments have been directly compared with general psychotherapy (e.g., Giles, 1983b; Giles & Hom, 1987; Giles, 1993; Kazdin & Wilson, 1980). More than 100 studies showing significant differences have been located. Two of these (Johnson & Greenberg, 1985; Snyder, Wills, & Grady-Fletcher, 1991)—both on marital therapy—favored traditional psychotherapy. The remainder of these studies favored directive techniques (Giles, Prial, & Neims, 1993). This finding documents the success of continuing research efforts to develop, test, and refine disorder-specific sets of intervention.

EXAMPLES OF STUDIES AND
METHODOLOGIES

An early comparative outcome study completed by Sloane, Staples, Cristol, Yorkston, and Whipple (1975) randomly assigned outpatients to insight-oriented psychotherapy, behavior therapy, or a minimal attention control. Other methodological strengths of this study, advanced for its time, included multiple measures of outcome, independent assessors blind to conditions, taped sessions (to determine whether treatments could indeed be discriminated by blind reviewers), three experienced therapists per treatment team, and long-term followups.

Although most of the comparisons between treatments yielded no significant differences, seven of the eight significant findings favored prescriptive techniques. For example, 93 percent of the behaviorally treated patients improved, compared to 77 percent of the patients treated with psychotherapy. (Also, 77 percent of the minimal treatment controls improved.) For a more in-depth review of the study, see Giles (1983a).

This was one of the beginning studies indicating a possible superiority of prescriptive psychotherapy. Similarly, a review by Luborsky, Singer, and Luborsky (1975) found that 6 out of 6 significant findings favored prescriptive therapy (versus 13 tie scores).

The Sloane study had several weaknesses, including lack of random assignment of therapists. In the Paul (1966) study, this problem was resolved by having each therapist provide both active treatments. In the Sloane study, however, each set of therapists practiced according to their respective specializations. This treatment-by-treatment team confound raises the challenge that results favoring prescriptive treatment were due not to the treatment itself but to the possibility that better therapists delivered it. (The behavior therapists were rated by patients in this study as significantly more empathetic than their psychotherapy counterparts.) The experimenters did not use multivarate statistical techniques to analyze results, thus inflating the probability that significant differences were due to chance. Using a general psychiatric population, the researchers also were unable to provide information from the study as to the applicability (or lack thereof) of the treatments to specific disorders. Much of the comparative outcome research subsequent to Sloane studied homogeneous disorders alone. This reduces error variance, encouraging true differences between treatments to emerge.

Miller, Norman, Keitner, Bishop, and Dow (1989) published one of the first comparative outcome studies of severely depressed inpatients. The comparison groups included standard psychotherapy/milieu treatment, cognitive therapy, and social skills training. Patients were randomly assigned to treatment groups in the hospital and provided the same treatment on an outpatient basis four months after discharge. Both the social skills and the cognitive therapy groups showed significantly more positive differences on the Beck Depression Inventory and SCL-90 measures of general symptomatology. These conditions also had greater numbers of treatment responders (80 percent versus 40 percent). The researchers utilized multivariate statistics, good selection criteria to ensure homogeneous groups, experienced therapists, analyses not only of responders but of dropouts, severely depressed clinical subjects, and tests for treatment integrity.

Drawbacks included a treatment-by-treatment team confound, a sample size too small to detect all true differences, and the observation of pretreatment statistical differences among conditions (which emerged despite randomization). This latter problem was handled sufficiently via the use of covariance, but this in turn complicated the interpretation of results. The finding of superiority of prescriptive treatment in this study is consistent with additional data from studies discussed under the depressive disorders section later in this chapter.

Kazdin, Esveldt-Dawson, French, and Unis (1987) compared problem-solving skills training and nondirective psychotherapy in the treatment of children hospitalized for antisocial behavior. The 56 subjects (11 girls and 45 boys, ages 5 through 13) were admitted for acute disorders, including highly aggressive and destructive behavior, suicidal or homicidal ideation or intent, extreme or deteriorating family conditions, fighting, stealing, running away, and truancy. In order to be included in the study, subjects needed to be rated by a parent at or above the 98th percentile on either the aggression or delinquency scale of the Child Behavior Checklist.

Subjects were randomly assigned to conditions and treated by experienced therapists who had participated in an intensive training program for six months to learn each treatment technique. Treatments were detailed in manual form, and supervision of therapists included direct observation of each session, review of session tapes, case discussion, and group supervision meetings. Therapists followed a treatment manual that detailed therapy on a session-by-session basis as well as checklists following each session that prescribed the necessary materials, themes, and techniques. Multivariate statistics were used. Dropout data were included along with a long-term (one-year) followup assessment. The experimenters used multiple, psychometrically adequate outcome measures and sophisticated indications of the clinical significance of the treatment (the extent to which treatments moved subjects within normative ranges on questionnaires). The experimenters also obtained therapist and client ratings of outcome.

Results showed that problem-solving therapy had significantly more positive effects than relationship therapy and limited-contact controls. These results were sustained at a one-year followup and were evident on measures both at home and at school. Children who had received problem-solving treatment

> evinced significant reductions in total behavioral problems at home and in school and improvements on measures of school performance rated by the parents and of overall school adjustment rated by the teacher. In contrast, children in the other groups made either few gains over the course of treatment and follow-up ... or became significantly worse on selected measures (the control group). (Kazdin et al., 1987)

The discussion below delineates further comparative information by specific disorders.

Bulimia Nervosa and Other Eating Disorders

Directive treatment for bulimia appears to have improved therapeutic outcome. This treatment includes self-monitoring of binge-purge episodes and of food intake, client ingestion of three meals per day, cognitive restructuring of body image distortion and low self-esteem, appropriate nutritional information, and, perhaps most importantly, an increasing diversity in the ingestion and metabolism of difficult (i.e., anxiety-provoking) foods (Giles, Young, & Young, 1985). Although an eating disorder per se, bulimia appears to be basically an anxiety disorder based on fear of gaining weight and oversensitivity to perceived rejection and social ridicule (e.g., Leitenberg, 1993).

This type of approach has been shown to be superior to experimental conditions inclusive of nonspecific treatment mechanisms (Craighead & Agras, 1991). It was superior in two comparisons to traditional psychotherapy (Kirkley, Schneider, Agras, & Bachman, 1985; Fairburn, Kirk, O'Connor, & Cooper, 1986). It was also superior to traditional treatment for distortion of body image (Dworkin & Kerr, 1987), a factor associated with both the etiology and successful treatment of bulimia (Rosen, 1990). Maintenance of directive treatment effects appears to be stable over followup periods as long as four years posttreatment (Craighead & Agras, 1991).

Results from pharmacologic studies indicate the superiority of antidepressant medication to placebo: purging decrements range between 50 and 91 percent, abstinence rates between 30 and 68 percent.

Although data on long-term treatment with medication is sparse, clinical reports indicate that maintenance effects are poor once medication is withdrawn (Pope, Hudson, Jonas, & Yurgelin-Todd, 1985). Antidepressant medication appears to work in a direction opposite to that of cognitive-behavioral interventions (i.e., by helping bulimics more successfully restrain their eating from difficult and/or forbidden foods; Craighead and Agras, 1991). This factor may explain the higher relapse rates with medication treatment.

Mitchell, Pyle, Elkert, Hatsukami, Pomeroy, and Zimmerman (1990) randomly assigned 174 bulimic women to one of four experimental conditions (imipramine or placebo crossed with cognitive-behavioral treatment or no treatment). The medication groups suffered significantly higher dropouts from treatment, probably due to side effects. This is not an uncommon finding and one that constitutes a disadvantage of this approach. The frequency of binge-purging improved in the imipramine condition relative to placebo; however, the directive treatment was superior to imipramine. In the combined treatment group, 51 percent of the patients were abstinent posttreatment, compared with 16 percent in the imipramine only group. "Overall, it is clear that imipramine added nothing to cognitive-behavioral treatment in terms of the main outcome measure, decrease in binge eating and purging, but it may have added significantly in terms of reduction of symptoms of anxiety and depression" (Mitchell et al., 1990, p. 122).

Directive treatment appears superior to traditional psychotherapy in the treatment of obesity as well (e.g., Craighead & Agras, 1991). This is a qualified finding since directive treatment effects reaching *and maintaining* clinical significance with this population are still difficult to achieve and rarely observed in the empirical literature (Brownell & Wadden, 1991). Also, managed mental health care benefits rarely cover psychological treatment of obesity. Unfortunately, no consistent superiority has yet been found for any of the various treatments for anorexia nervosa. (Several encouraging studies, however, are ongoing; David Garner, personal communication, 1991).

A more extensive review of the comparative outcome literature on the treatment of bulimia nervosa is available in Leitenberg (1993).

Unipolar Depression

The most common finding in studies of traditional psychotherapy of depression is that it does not induce treatment effects superior to placebo (Covi, Lipman, Derogatis, Smith, & Pattison, 1974; Friedman, 1975; Klerman, DiMascio, Weissman, Prusoff, & Paykel, 1974). Fairly clear and consistent superiority to placebo has, however, been demonstrated for directive treatment such as interpersonal psychotherapy, cognitive-behavior therapy, and cognitive therapy. In addition to the Miller and associates' (1989) study, there are 10 studies favoring directive over traditional treatments for this disorder (Bellack, Hersen, & Himmelhoch, 1983; Covi & Lipman, 1987; Gallagher & Thompson, 1982; LaPointe & Rimm, 1980; Lerner & Clum, 1990; Lieberman & Eckman, 1981; McLean & Hakstian, 1979; 1990; Morris, 1978; Nezu, 1986; Steur, Mintz, Hammen, Hill, Jarvik, McCarley, Motoike, & Rosen, 1984).

A meta-analytic review (Dobson, 1989) reported that effect sizes from cognitive therapy were significantly greater than those induced by placebo and other treatments.

Directive treatments for this disorder typically focus on the identification and correction of irrational cognitions, training in social skills, increased social interaction, increased pleasurable activities, daily logging of automatic thoughts (and of their cognitive correction), behavioral homework assignments designed to increase the client's sense of self-efficacy, and assertiveness training. Experienced practitioners make sure to rule out competing factors such as medical illness or anxiety disorders (e.g., Beck et al., 1979; Wolpe, 1986).

The comparison of treatment effects of directive with medication therapy is more difficult to interpret. Although the Dobson (1989) review and several comparative studies found that directive treatment was superior, the most extensive and methodologically sophisticated study on this issue to date, the NIMH Treatment of Depression Collaborative Research Project (Elkin, Parloff, Hadley, & Autry, 1985), found medication treatment to be superior to interpersonal psychotherapy and to cognitive therapy, especially for severely depressed patients with a predominance of vegetative signs. (Beck, 1991, however, reported that results at long-term followup favored cognitive therapy.) The individual studies indicating superiority of directive treatment to medication all suffered methodological deficiencies, raising concerns that the medication treatment might not have been properly implemented (Hollon, Shelton, & Loosen, 1991). There may be a slight superiority derived from the combination of directive with pharmacologic treatment, but to date this effect has been small and difficult to replicate (Hollon, Shelton, & Loosen, 1991). Resolution of these issues awaits additional data.

There is indication that directive treatment yields better maintenance effects compared to pharmacotherapy. Hollon and Najavits (1988) reviewed five published studies indicating greater prophylactic effects. Whether this effect is due to treatment prophylaxis or to differential retention effects (see Hollon, Shelton, & Loosen, 1991) also awaits further study.

Conduct/Oppositional Disorder

Antisocial and conduct problems among children and adolescents cause managed care headaches on a consistent basis. These problems seem to comprise yet another area of mental health care where provider promises exceed the implications of empirical data. There is little evidence, for example, of comparative efficacy of the inpatient approach. Parents convinced otherwise, however, may pressure managed care to provide lengthy inpatient stays for adolescents who are very difficult to control.

Conduct/oppositional disorders are difficult to treat, and success rates across outpatient and inpatient treatments are not particularly impressive. As the age of the conduct-disordered or oppositional child increases from 8 to 17, success rates decline (Gerald Patterson, personal communication, 1991). Empirical findings document moderately encouraging results for some approaches and results ranging from neutral to dismal for others. In the Alexander studies (Alexander & Parsons, 1973; Parsons & Alexander, 1973), for example, in which directive treatment, Rogerian treatment, and psychodynamic treatment were compared with themselves and with no-treatment controls, only the directive therapy (a combination of parent training, family/systems interventions, and contingency management) yielded superior results. Compared to no treatment, the Rogerian approach did not distinguish itself, and the psychodynamically treated patients showed significantly worrisome rates of deterioration. This emphasizes the point that type of treatment may make crucial differences in outcomes by disorder.

Patterson and associates have published and comprised substantive literature on these problems over the past 20 years (e.g., Patterson, Chamberlain, & Dishion, 1993; Patterson, Chamberlain, & Reid, 1992). Patterson's work uses parent training, contingency management, and school intervention, and, like the Alexander studies, appears to have comparative superiority to traditional psychotherapy in outcome research (e.g., Patterson, Chamberlain, & Reid, 1992). Treatment process emphasizes microanalysis of coercive family interactions, which, in the absence of treatment, tend to escalate violence, truancy, stealing, and general family disruption.

Training aids are available for interested therapists, and several manuals have been published both as treatment aids to clinicians and as learning aids to parents (Forgatch & Patterson, 1989; Patterson & Forgatch, 1987). Although family therapy interventions are preferred for these conditions, individual-directive approaches, applied in institutional settings when intact families were unavailable, were apparently superior both to nonspecific mechanisms and to alternative treatments (Kazdin et al., 1987; Kazdin, Bass, Siegel, & Thomas, 1989; Kendall,

Reber, McLeer, Epps, & Ronan, 1990; Michelson, Mannacino, Marchione, Stern, Figueroa, & Beck, 1983).

Consistent with these studies, a study by Szapocznik, Murray, Scopetta, Hervis, Rio, Cohen, Rivas-Vasquez, and Posada (1989) found brief, structural family therapy superior to psychodynamic child therapy for Hispanic boys suffering from severe behavioral problems. These studies may provide treatment models for therapist-entrepreneurs wishing to attract managed care's referral business.

Schizophrenia

The advent of neuroleptic drugs constituted a major advance in the treatment of schizophrenic illness. Less widely recognized is literature indicating that directive treatments have relatively superior outcome to placebo and to traditional treatments in the management of this disease. Ironically (but typically), however, it is the less efficacious psychodynamic treatment approach which is implemented most often with such patients (e.g., Feinsilver, 1983, 1986; Kernberg, 1986; Lassers, 1986; Mann, 1986; Munich, 1987; Strean, 1988; see Mueser & Berenbaum, 1990, for review).

Although the present chapter is provided primarily to document brief-treatment efficacy (as opposed to criticizing opposing orientations), a bit more space will be taken here to discuss the utilization of psychodynamic treatment for schizophrenia due to Mueser and Berenbaum's (1990) call for a moratorium on this approach. These authors cite four recent studies in which psychodynamic treatment was compared with other approaches (milieu, drug treatment, directive treatment, or some combination) with schizophrenic patients. Three of the four studies found that psychodynamic treatment failed to exert any beneficial outcome either alone or in combination with antipsychotic medication. The fourth study, which Mueser and Berenbaum deemed uninterpretable due to methodological weaknesses, indicated a modest beneficial effect of psychodynamic care. These authors also cited naturalistic studies, indicating that such treatment leads to deleterious outcomes with some schizophrenic patients: higher rates of suicide, lengthy hospitalization, rehospitalization, unemployment, initial inpatient admits, and relationship discord.

Such findings contrast to the outcome of studies on the efficacy of social skills training (Bellack, Turner, Hersen, & Luber, 1984; Gunderson, Frank, Katz, Vannicelli, Frosch, & Knapp, 1984; Hogarty, Anderson, Reiss, Kornblith, Greenwald, Jauna, & Madonia, 1986; Lieberman, Mueser, & Wallace, 1986) as well as with certain types of family therapy for schizophrenia (Falloon & Pederson, 1985; Hogarty et al., 1986; Leff,

Kuipers, Berkowitz, & Sturgeon, 1982). For example, Lieberman, Mueser and Wallace (1986) found that, at two-year followup after postinpatient discharge, schizophrenics receiving nine weeks of social skills training had significantly better social functioning, less severe symptomatology, and less inpatient treatment than schizophrenics receiving holistic health care. (Both groups received neuroleptics as well.) Hogarty and colleagues (1986) found that none of the schizophrenics who received both family therapy and social skills therapy relapsed over one year, compared to 20 percent receiving either therapy alone and 41 percent receiving supportive psychotherapy alone. Two-year relapse rates were 25 percent for the combination treatment versus 66 percent for the supportive psychotherapy condition.

Falloon and colleagues (Falloon & Pederson, 1985; Falloon, McGill, Boyd, & Pederson, 1987) reported that 17 percent of schizophrenic patients treated for two years with directive (behavioral) family therapy relapsed, compared to 83 percent of patients treated with individual supportive psychotherapy. Gunderson and colleagues (1984) randomly assigned schizophrenic patients to exploratory, insight-oriented, psycho-dynamic (EIO) treatment or to reality-adaptive supportive (RAS) therapy which was

> focused on problems in the current living situation of the patient. In con-
> trast to the EIO therapy, there was little attempt to explore the past and to
> seek correlates between past experience and the present. Rather, the explo-
> ration of the present was intended to identify problems that could be
> solved or that could be expected to recur in the future so that more effec-
> tive coping strategies could be mapped out. Another major feature of the
> RAS therapy was its focus on the patient's behavior itself rather than the
> covert meanings behind that behavior. (Stanton, Gunderson, Knapp, Frank,
> Vanicelli, Schnitzer, & Rosenthal, 1984, p. 535)

Gunderson and associates found that EIO was inferior to RAS for rates of rehospitalization, vocational adjustment, and social adjustment.

Additional studies showing the superiority of directive to tradi-tional therapy for schizophrenia include King, Armitage, and Tilton (1960), Hartlage (1970), Ney, Palvesky, and Markely, (1971), Paul and Lentz (1977), and Schwartz and Bellack (1975).

Obsessive-Compulsive Disorder

The impact of directive treatments has been most widely acknowledged for the anxiety disorders. Early detractors of brief therapy acknowledged its superiority for treatment of simple phobia (e.g., Luborsky, Singer, & Luborsky, 1975). Since this time, however, directive (primarily behavioral or cognitive-behavioral) treatments have been studied in an extensive literature and have appeared to gain treatments-of-choice status across the gamut of such problems. The complex and treatment-resistant area of obsessive-compulsive disorder provides a good example of this research.

The majority of obsessive-compulsive patients are either washers or checkers. Washers fear contamination and wash to an extensive, often debilitating, extent once they perceive that their efforts to avoid contaminants have failed. Checkers fear catastrophe and engage in elaborate checking rituals, also to a debilitating extent, to ensure against catastrophic oversight.

Until the advent of exposure with response prevention in the 1970s (see Rachman & Hodgson, 1980, for review), there was no successful treatment for obsessive-compulsive disorder. Discouragements were the result of treatments ranging from systematic desensitization to psychoanalysis, from neuroleptics to psychosurgery.

Exposure treatments for obsessive-compulsive disorder formed the basis for the new treatments for bulimia nervosa (discussed earlier). For example, washers are given 24-hour exposure to a graduated hierarchy of feared contaminants/situations. In general, they are not allowed to wash or shower except during supervised periods of the day. These supervised wash periods are followed immediately by "recontamination." Other treatments, such as assertiveness training, relationship therapy, and cognitive therapy, are applied as indicated by each particular case. Imaginal flooding techniques are used to supplement direct exposure, appearing to enhance long-term maintenance of results (e.g. Foa, Steketee, & Milby, 1980).

At present, exposure with response prevention is the only extant psychological treatment with extratherapeutic effects for this disorder. Response rates range from 60 to 75 percent with fairly good long-term maintenance. This treatment has been shown to be superior to nonspecific factors (e.g., Foa, Steketee, & Milby, 1980; Marks, 1982; Milby & Meredith, 1980) and to traditional psychotherapy (Moreno, 1981).

An exciting and interesting advance in obsessive-compulsive treatment has been observed with clinical trials of new medications, notably Clomipramine (about 40 percent of obsessive-compulsive patients find improvement or significant improvement from medication treatment alone). However, there are problems associated with side effects and with high relapse rates once medication is withdrawn. The possibility of enhancement effects for the combination of exposure/response prevention with medication management awaits the outcome of several ongoing empirical trials. Regular tricyclic medication has been shown to enhance the efficacy of exposure/response prevention for obsessive-compulsive patients who are severely depressed. Directive treatment may in turn enhance the stability of treatment gains once medication is withdrawn. A more complete review of this literature, discussing comparative outcome both with psychotherapy and with medications, is available in Steketee (1993).

Panic Disorder

Panic disorder is the most extensively studied of the anxiety disorders, especially with regard to responsiveness to prescriptive techniques. This literature warrants here a more extensive discussion of the nature and treatment of this disorder.

Anxiety disorders are the most prevalent of the clinical\psychiatric dysfunctions (Weissman & Merikangas, 1986). Panic disorder, either with or without agoraphobic avoidance, is also associated with high prevalence as well as with additional morbidity such as depression, suicide, substance abuse, benzodiazepine addiction, generalized anxiety disorder, other phobias (especially social phobia), and marital discord (Markowitz, Weissman, Ouelette, Lish, & Klereman, 1989). Directive treatment for this disorder utilizes exposure treatment as its core element. Research since the early 1960s has been devoted to the development of additional treatment components which add to exposure-induced effects.

In many cases, panic disorder appears to be due to a misattribution of anxiety symptoms: The client expects that symptoms such as tachycardia, parethesia, dizziness, dyspnea, and/or chest pain will lead to some imminent catastrophe (heart attack, social embarrassment, losing control, going insane). Specialists in panic disorder treatment rule out medical problems with similar symptomatology (limbic lobe seizures, mitral valve prolapse, hypoglycemia, caffeine toxification, adrenal tumor, hyperthyroidism). Recent research on hyperventilatory syndrome (Ley, 1987) suggests that an assessment of respiration rates should be made because the symptoms of hyperventilatory hypocapnia also mimic those of panic disorder.

Patients suffering from panic disorder without agoraphobia are fairly easily and successfully treated with one of two directive therapy techniques. Barlow's (e.g., Barlow & Cerny, 1988) method involves relaxation training, cognitive restructuring, breathing retraining, and systematic exposure to interoceptive cues. While conceptually similar, the cognitive therapy approach places greater emphasis on the cognitive and behavioral correction of the patient's anxiety misattributions. Both methods yield success rates of about 95 percent with good stability and end-point functioning at long-term followup (Barlow & Cerny, 1988; Sokol,

Beck, Greenberg, Berchick, & Wright, 1989a, 1989b). These methods are the treatments of choice for panic disorder without agoraphobia (Clum, 1989).

Agoraphobic clients are generally more difficult to treat, have less impressive success rates, are somewhat more prone to relapse, and generally have a more complicated clinical picture (Clum, 1989). Also more likely with these clients are problems associated with medication management and withdrawal (which will be discussed).

Exposure also appears to be critical to successful psychological treatment of this condition. Clients are asked to approach a hierarchy of feared situations and to stay in these situations—often accompanied by the therapist—until anxiety significantly declines. Studies indicate that the efficacy of this treatment is bolstered by therapist-assisted exposure, long durations of exposure, frequent practice, and the administration of the exposure treatment in group format (e.g., Michelson & Marchione, 1991).

Significant improvement rates with agoraphobics typically range between 50 and 60 percent, including dropouts. Long-term maintenance rates are good. The typical treatment-responsive client has made further gains at posttreatment followups ranging up to nine years. Successfully treated patients, however, still tend to have some residual problems.

Additional therapy components such as paradoxical intention (Ascher, 1981) tend to add to exposure's effects. Although in need of replication, the most promising study to date (Michelson, Marchione, & Greenwald, 1989) showed that the addition of cognitive therapy (identification and validity testing of faulty beliefs, use of Socratic dialogue, problem solving, reattribution, and generalization programming) to graduated exposure resulted in 86 percent of subjects reaching high end-point functioning. Results maintained at three-month followup. The researchers stated that cognitive therapy, combined with graduated exposure, "is the most effective treatment we have developed or tested to date at our center. This includes a decade of clinical research, during which time we have examined pharmacologic, behavioral, and various cognitive interventions."

There are several dozen studies available that demonstrate the superiority of this treatment to placebo/nonspecific controls. There are also several clinical trials showing its superiority to traditional treatment (e.g., Cooper, Gelder, & Marks, 1965; Gelder, Bancroft, Gath, Johnston, Mathews, & Shaw, 1973; Gelder & Marks, 1968; Gelder, Marks, & Wolff, 1967; Gillan & Rachman, 1974).

Medications may also be quite useful for this problem but tend to be associated with a number of issues that should be carefully considered before implementation. The "gold standard" for treatment of panic disorder with agoraphobia is that obtained by the tricyclic, imipramine. A range of other tricyclics and monoamine oxidase inhibitors (MAOIs) have been tried with relatively similar results (for a more in-depth discussion, see Clum, 1989; Michelson & Marchione, 1991). Tricyclic treatment will result in significant and fairly immediate improvement among 30 to 55 percent of agoraphobic clients. However, such medications are refused by 20 percent, and dropout rates add another 25 to 35 percent (apparently due to side effects that mimic panic symptoms).

Relapse rates of 35 to 60 percent are regularly reported once medication is withdrawn. MAOIs are considered tertiary alternatives due to problems with toxicity and special problems with side effects. Low-potency benzodiazapines (e.g., Valium) are also considered tertiary since these drugs have not consistently enhanced treatment effects and have high tendencies to induce psychological dependence, tolerance, side effects, and relapse.

Despite encouraging results in initial reports, the use of high-potency benzodiazapines such as alprazolam (Xanax) should also be considered a tertiary alternative. Despite fewer problems with side effects and slightly higher significant improvement rates, Balinger (1990) reported that many clients in phase one of the Upjohn collaborative panic study could not be withdrawn from the drug due to psychological dependence. Of those discontinuing the medication, 30 percent suffered rebound panic attacks worse than those for which treatment was originally sought. Finally, 90 percent of these clients relapsed following drug withdrawal. Klosko, Barlow, Tassinari, and Cerny (1990) found that directive psychological intervention caused 80 percent of clients to be panic free at posttreatment, compared with 50 percent treated by Xanax.

The disadvantages associated with Xanax are counterbalanced to an extent by its rapid onset of effects (one to two weeks), high compliance and acceptance rates, low attrition, and reductions not only in panic attacks but in more generalized anxiety states (46 percent of clients) at dosages of 2 to 3 mg/day (Balinger, 1990).

Such data have led Clum (1989) to conclude that directive psychological therapies for panic disorder are currently the treatments of choice. Such treatments, however, are more stressful than drug treatments due to the necessity of asking clients to endure exposure to their fears. They also require more time, more effort, and more of a waiting period before treatment effects are observed.

As with bulimia, pharmacologic and directive treatments of panic disorder tend to work by mechanisms that are not necessarily compatible. Drug treatment is aimed toward "blocking" panic attacks (although the actual mechanism of drug treatment is far from clear—see Telch, Agras, Taylor, Roth, & Gallen, 1985). Directive treatment, on the other hand, teaches panic-disordered patients not to avoid but to cope with fear—and eventually to perceive it to be safe from catastrophe. Clum's (1989) review indicated that the addition of directive treatment to medication treatment reduced relapse and enhanced outcome over that seen with drug regimens alone. However, the addition of drug treatment to directive treatment tended to reduce treatment outcome over that observed with directive treatment alone. It is recommended (Michelson & Marchione, 1991) that clinicians provide clients with information about the advantages and disadvantages of each approach and then collaborate with clients in order to facilitate treatment choice.

Other Anxiety Disorders

Although data for additional disorders are either less consistent or more nascent than for the disorders discussed above, trends favoring directive treatment are also evident for generalized anxiety disorder (GAD) and posttraumatic stress disorder (PTSD). Recent trials of cognitive therapy for GAD (e.g., Butler, Fennell, Robson, & Gelder, 1991; Durham & Turvey, 1987) indicated its superiority to nonspecific treatment effects. Although tie scores have been observed in some studies on GAD comparing directive with traditional psychotherapy, all studies showing significant differences have favored directive techniques (Borkovec, Mathews, Chambers, Ebrahami, Lytle, & Nelson, 1987). It should be noted that Borkovec's results favoring directive treatment did not replicate in a subsequent study by this research team (Borkovec & Mathews, 1988). Thus, further data are needed to establish with confidence a recommendation of cognitive/directive treatment for this disorder.

Outcome research on PTSD is in a relatively early stage. Available research, however (e.g., Cooper & Clum, 1989), reports superiority of directive over traditional treatments. For a more complete review of outcome research on this disorder, see Blake, Abueg, Woodward, and Keane (1993).

The above review does not completely report the relevant number of available outcome studies—or the number of disorders—in which brief, directive treatments have appeared to gain a comparative advantage to date. In addition to the disorders discussed, more complete reviews of this nature are available for enuresis, autism, developmental disability, borderline personality disorder, social phobia, and other disorders in a handbook of chapters compiled by the author (Giles, 1993).

OTHER PROMISING BRIEF-
TREATMENT APPROACHES

The promise of behavioral and cognitive-behavioral techniques is mitigated to a degree by a number of drawbacks. The first is the lack of relative popularity of these approaches. For example, the surveys previously
cited indicate that only 10 to 25 percent of practitioners utilize behavioral
or cognitive-behavioral methods primarily. Fewer still stay abreast of
current research or use it to guide their practice techniques (Giles, 1993).

Second, many cases that present to managed care are not "disorder-
specific." Instead, they compromise an admixture of a variety of clinical
and subclinical concerns that vary along a wide continuum of severity of
disturbance. Although a number of behavioral models (e.g., Wolpe, 1990)
are available that are capable of handling such exigencies, these more
individualized approaches have received only modest investigation.

Finally, it should be noted that cognitive and behavioral techniques,
though more efficient than traditional psychotherapies, have not yet
attended to the high dropout data indicating that consumers, in large
degree, prefer treatment approaches that begin and terminate within 10
sessions or less (Pekarik, 1993). Such deficits open the managed care door
to brief-treatment approaches spawned from quite different theoretical
orientations.

A particularly impressive approach to brief therapy has been
developed by the systems, strategic, and Ericksonian schools (e.g., de
Shazer, 1985; Haley, 1973; Watzlawick, Weakland, & Fish, 1974).
Proponents of these schools write persuasively and in a manner that
invites implementation by therapists of many different training back-
grounds. Many of the reported models of treatment work in 6 to 10 sessions of intervention. Although these treatments were at first difficult for
practitioners to assimilate, more recent efforts have delineated a variety
of concepts central to the approach (e.g., de Shazer, 1985).

In general, these therapies tend to be advice giving but nonjudg-
mental. The general theme is of indirection, paradoxical homework
assignments, and the use of seemingly innocuous verbal and nonverbal
communications to set the context for change. Strategic theorists have
been particularly attuned to the problem of premature dropout and the
need for quick, effective intervention. Treatment methods seem
particularly applicable, from a managed care sense, to the numerous
"general" cases that appear in the intake offices of managed care
assessors.

Since the field, albeit with some reluctance, is moving slowly but
surely toward empiricism, it is hoped that the above theorists and their
followers will begin outcome research. This will enable those in the field
to eventually have an indication as to the comparative effectiveness of

these techniques and their applicability (or lack thereof) to the gamut of the emotional disorders.

Another promising approach is that described by Garfield (1989). Garfield's emphasis is on eclecticism—the orientation preferred most frequently by practitioners. Garfield included a comprehensive and promising review of research on brief therapy. He also reviewed the history of the brief-therapy movement beginning with Rank's departure from classical psychoanalysis in the 1920's.

Garfield's approach, similar to many brief-therapy procedures, recommends: (1) identifying—with the aid of the client—treatment goals that are observable, measurable, and specific to the task at hand; (2) implementing a therapeutic style that is active and directive; (3) utilizing techniques that have research validation; and (4) tailoring treatment interventions to match the specific needs of each client. Interestingly, this approach bears striking resemblance to that recommended by prominent behavior therapists (e.g., Wolpe, 1990).

Garfield also paid attention to the consumer preference literature, citing research that clients' perceptions of therapy at the third visit (but, curiously, not at the first) correlate well with eventual outcome. He also cited research confuting the presumption of symptom substitution as well as studies that indicate that missed appointments (but not canceled appointments) correlate significantly with premature dropouts. Another positive feature of this approach is its use of validated questionnaires—from therapist, observer, and patient perspectives—for the measurement of therapeutic outcome. This approach is also quite compatible with managed care.

Ironically, the most prolific contributor to brief-therapy styles has been from the impetus of psychoanalysis: Dynamic therapies alone represent more than 20 different types of brief-therapy interventions (Garfield, 1989). Of these approaches, Luborsky's (e.g., Luborsky, 1984) has the most empirical validation. For example, Luborsky and his colleagues found that a positive therapeutic alliance was especially instrumental to eventual outcome. They also found that the accuracy of interpretation, based primarily on the core conflictual relationship theme (CCRT), correlated significantly with eventual outcome. An instrument has been developed that measures the CCRT reliably well.

The CCRT identifies three features: what the patient wants from the persons discussed in session narratives, how these persons are expected to respond, and how the patient responds. The CCRT is the first reliable measure describing rules that dynamically oriented therapists follow when they interpret for patients the deeper meaning of various relationships. Although the CCRTs tend to remain stable throughout the therapy process, positive outcome is associated both with patients' responses and their expected responses of others.

Dynamically oriented therapists will find Luborsky's approach amenable to the requirements of many managed health care systems. (It has been adapted to a 20-session or less model.) As with many of the dynamic therapies, there is currently little information on Luborsky's approach with reference to comparative outcome, effectiveness by disorder, and so forth. However, there is an ongoing trail attempting to determine whether or not the CCRT will add to the efficacy of behavior therapy for the treatment of panic disorder with agoraphobia (Ralph M. Turner, personal communication, 1991).

References to additional brief–therapy approaches can be found in Garfield (1989).

Chapter 9

Legal and Ethical Concerns

Managed care represents a new playing field for the application of established ethical principles and judicial precedents. Few of the published ethical/legal guidelines appear relevant to the unique concerns of managed care's cost-containment emphasis. A literature on both areas of interest, however, is developing.

ETHICAL GUIDELINES

The American Psychological Association (1990) formalized a set of ethical criteria that may be relevant to managed mental health care settings (Haas & Cummings, 1991). To avoid patient abandonment, for example, mental health professionals must treat patients until presenting problems are satisfactorily cleared, a referral is made, or care is terminated. This becomes a thorny issue when the patient runs out of benefits and requests/needs further care. Unless a referral can be made, the therapist is ethically, if not legally, obligated to provide care. Many providers deal with this exigency by reserving private practice slots for discounted-fee or *pro bono* patients, and they restrict the number of HMO referrals they accept for patients who seem in need of long-term care. These concerns apply to managed care staff models as well. The Biodyne model does not restrict the number of outpatient sessions, and some other HMO benefits extend to $2,000 or 50 visits per year. Both of these situations are unusual, however. The typical coverage is 20 visits or $1,000.

The denial of appropriate care presents substantial ethical (and legal) difficulties. Critics of capitated systems have been principally concerned with this possibility because the fiscal incentive associates a decrease in delivered services with an increase in profit (Armenti, 1991).

This is indeed a valid concern, and managed care systems, as the next section on legal issues documents, have apparently made serious

120

errors in this regard. On the other hand, it would be inaccurate to conclude that such abuses are rampant due to the nature of the deterrents to
care denial. The inappropriate denial of outpatient care, for instance,
may too often lead to the need for more intensive (and expensive) treatment down the road. Inpatients discharged inappropriately soon risk
repeated readmissions with all the clinical problems and expense these
entail.

Inappropriate denial risks acquaintance with a number of other
consequences. The frequency of complaints rises, leading to greater ten-
sion among corporate staff. Should the complaints be resolved inadequately, they transfer to a higher level (i.e., the health plan or employer
responsible for the hire of the managed care company's services).
Inappropriate denial is one of the quickest ways to ruin for a managed
care company because the hiring entity becomes dissatisfied and fails to
renew the contract. In such instances, other unhappy entities become
involved: the insurance commissioner, the EAP, the state grievance
board, community providers, and prosecuting attorneys (Giles, 1989).
Managed care representatives find such difficulties to be quite
frustrating, time consuming, and anxiety provoking.

Ethical guidelines mandate the provision of services for which
providers are qualified by training and experience. In the author's experience, many providers attempt to gain membership to PPO/HMO
panels by advertising brief therapy skills for which they are not adequately trained. As managed care systems continue their trend toward
increasing sophistication, formal training in brief-therapeutic techniques
will be made part of the credentialing process for therapists. Therapists
are well advised to obtain formal training and certification in this crucial
area.

Therapist-employees of managed care systems wrestle with com-
plexities involved in the interpretation of ethical guidelines for conflict of
interest and dual relationships. Subsidiary employees wear two hats, one
for therapy and one for insurance. This entails a juggling act between the
provision of care and its cost. In such systems there is good possibility of
confusion as to principal fidelity. On the one hand, therapists are
expected to provide services at costs meeting projected medical ratios
determined by capitation-driven budgets. On the other hand, they face
multitudes of seriously disturbed individuals in need of psychological
care. This conceptual conflict points to one of the disadvantages of capitation: In a financial sense, the entity providing service is pitted against
the individuals in need of it.

The attempt to resolve this conflict usually resides with the placement of patient care before financial concerns—but with the
understanding that care is driven by medical necessity. Brief, goal-

directed treatment is provided on an outpatient basis, and crisis inter-
vention/stabilization is delivered on the hospital ward. In service to the
patient mandate, reputable managed mental health care systems work to
ensure that quality of care meets the highest professional standards. In
service to the corporate mandate, they also attempt to ensure that such
service is delivered to the appropriate level of care—no more and no less.

Therapists both internal and external to managed care systems are
ethically bound to ensure that their clients have adequate informed consent about benefits and expectations for care. This includes adequate disclosure about goal-driven therapy with concomitant time and economic
constraints.

The ethical principal of fidelity (Beauchamp & Childress, 1988; also
see Ethical Principals of Psychologists, APA, 1990) subsumes provider
loyalty to contractors (inclusive of managed care companies). If therapists do not feel loyal to managed care philosophy, they should refrain
from provider membership. Otherwise, they tend to impart a patient-
managed care split from which many subsequent problems ensue. As
Haas and Cummings stated, "To act otherwise is to risk colluding with
the patient and 'acting out' against the plan" (1991, p. 50).

Ethical guidelines indicate that professionals should communicate
first with each other about known or suspected ethical violations or other
examples of inappropriate clinical behavior. As indicated elsewhere in
this book, psychiatric, psychological, and EAP organizations, feeling
intruded upon by the advent of managed care, have often neglected this
principle in favor of the placement of complaints to empowered third
parties (employers, grievance boards, insurance commissioners, and
attorneys). Ethical principals might justify such efforts should direct
communications, carefully documented, fail to obtain satisfaction.

Confidentiality issues present additional ethical concern to managed care systems. With the advancing sophistication of management
information systems, each patient—by diagnosis, by services rendered,
by disposition—can be pulled from the computer for review. Some managed mental health care companies are embedded within a larger HMO
structure, making the potential for access to such information much
greater. Staffing requirements for such companies can be very substantial, and (again) the possible access to confidential information by non-
clinical affiliates is great. Although this issue has attracted no legal action
and little ethical discussion to date, it presents a strong potential for difficulties that managed care should work hard to avoid.

The American Psychological Association's Counsel of
Representatives adopted a policy statement on managed mental health
care in 1988. The statement indicated that managed care frequently
imposes artificial and/or economic barriers to consumer access and that

it, by emphasizing short-term or biomedical intervention, may unfairly exclude those with greatest need. The statement went on to imply that managed care places too great an emphasis on short-term outpatient care and that it should strive to provide treatment with sufficient quality based on the available scientific evidence of efficacy.

While the point on treatment access is well taken, the APA's criticism of brief treatment is open to interpretation. The APA has been associated with advocacy of long-term, insight-oriented treatments without known scientific efficacy. It has seemed to promote the equivalence of therapies hypothesis (Giles, 1990b) and has actively resisted the inclusion of other ethical principles and/or guidelines recommending treatment based on scientific research (Hayes, 1987). The APA's differences with empirically oriented psychologists led to their secession from the organization and their subsequent formation of the American Psychological Society (Giles, 1990b). Thus the APA's motivations for recommending research-validated therapies, given the context in which these statements appeared, may well be viewed by managed care representatives with a degree of skepticism or distrust.

LEGAL ISSUES

The emergence of HMOs has left many legal questions in this area unanswered or as yet unchallenged. Nevertheless, a small but important literature has developed and will be reviewed here.

The author is not an attorney. The following information should not be construed as legal advice. The information is, however, derived from certain legal review sources (e.g., *Loss Prevention Letter, Practice and Liability Consultants*) as well as the actual literature itself. In order to provide an adequate review of the last two cases below (*Wickline* and *Wilson*), the author consulted an attorney who specializes in health care litigation.

The *Wickline* and *Wilson* cases indicate that legal precedents established for health care may be used by attorneys to argue cases involving managed mental health care. The following brief review thus includes some of the legal literature on health care suits against HMOs.

A particularly important legal concern regards the provision of treatment in accordance with community standards of care. Standard of care guidelines are written to urge clinicians to apply treatments with acceptable quality. The *Loss Prevention Letter* stated, "In the event of a lawsuit, would it be difficult to find a majority of reputable physicians willing to testify on your behalf that you performed in a manner most physicians in your specialty would perform?" (vol. V, issue 3). Such issues become thorny in communities where managed care presents a minority view on the management of inpatient or outpatient care.

The community standards issue was illustrated by the *Loss Prevention Letter* in a case that occurred in southern California. A radiologist calculated radiation dose manually because the patient's insurance did not pay for computerized tomography. (Computerized tomography was the standard of care.) An application error was made, which resulted in a tumor and blindness. The patient stated that he would have borne the extra charges for computerized tomography had he known the risks. A confidential settlement was reached in this case.

This case illuminates the necessity to obtain "informed refusal" from patients in need of treatments not covered by their insurance. Informed refusal should be carefully documented or, preferably, obtained in writing with the patient's signature. This case has obvious implications to the practice of inpatient and outpatient mental health care. The patient in this case did not sue his insurance company, leaving open the question of insurance liability when standard of care for a particular condition is not included within a benefit package.

Managed mental health care systems may be liable should they refer patients to providers whose treatment leads to unsatisfactory outcome. This is especially the case when managed care has prior knowledge about the provider's incompetence or impairment. While this issue mainly pertains to HMOs, individual providers also incur liability when they refuse a referral and instead recommend another provider within the panel. If the case turns out badly, and if the provider had prior knowledge of clinician impairment, a successful suit could result. HMOs will be particularly vulnerable to this problem should it be proven that their referrals are influenced more by provider discounts than by provider quality. This standard points to the necessity of having an adequate credentialing procedure and for promptly deleting a provider when problematic information becomes known and verified.

Psychiatric patients often come to closed panels requesting care from a specialist who is not on the list. This request is typically denied and an in-house referral made, raising a question of legal viability of closed panels, especially when an internal specialist is unavailable. This area also involves the use of informed refusal (i.e., informing the patient of the option of paying for the specialist's services out of pocket).

Some managed mental health care organizations withhold a portion of clinicians' fees against the possibility of excess medical costs during a calendar year. If the clinician group does not incur excess costs, then some or all of the withhold is returned. In some plans, a portion of the withhold is determined by the cost of specialty referrals.

Clinicians and managed care firms should be wary of this arrangement and should scrupulously avoid the denial of proper specialty referrals based primarily on cost. To do otherwise is to risk suit for negligence. Several suits of this nature have occurred against physicians apparently influenced too heavily by the withhold disincentive (*Loss Prevention Letter*, volume V, issue 3). In these and in other such cases, it is recommended that clinicians practice according to community standards regardless of reimbursement.

There is a small but growing literature on the patient's right to effective psychotherapeutic care. In 1988, the Wisconsin Supreme Court in *Schuster* v. *Altenberg* found that "negligent failure to diagnose or properly treat a psychiatric condition may constitute cause-in-fact of harm to the patient and third parties *if it can be established that with proper care, the patient's condition and behavior could have been corrected or controlled*" (p. 162, emphasis added). A 1985 Massachusetts case, *Stepakoff* v. *Kantar*, stipulated that therapists must take into account advances in the profession in the care and treatment of mentally or emotionally ill individuals.

In 1988, *Littleton* v. *Good Samaritan Hospital* (Ohio) brought further substantive interest to this area. Dr. Littleton was treated for depression on an inpatient basis at Good Samaritan. The principal mode of treatment was psychoanalytic intervention. The patient, unsatisfied with his progress at Good Samaritan, retained a psychiatrist who treated him (with good results) with antidepressant medication. The patient subsequently sued Good Samaritan for giving him a treatment of unproven efficacy in place of one of proven efficacy. This case was settled out of court. In addition to issues of competence, welfare of the consumer, and informed consent, these court cases illustrate the liability risks of clinician failure to keep abreast of current, empirically validated therapeutic procedures.

The last two cases, *Wickline* v. *State of California* and *Wilson* v. *Blue Cross of Southern California*, also have fairly direct bearing on managed mental health care practice. Lois Wickline sued MediCal, the California Medicaid program, alleging that her early discharge from the hospital caused her to lose her leg from postsurgical complications. Her physician had requested an eight-day inpatient extension following aorto-femoral bypass surgery. The extension was denied despite the physician's prediction that a thrombus in the artery might eventually lead to amputation. Wickline sued MediCal, but not her physician, and lost her case on appeal.

Despite this outcome, the *Wickline* case established liability for both physician and third-party payer in case of adverse outcome following utilization review. The judge ruled:

> Third party payors of health care services can be held legally accountable when medically inappropriate decisions result from defects in cost containment mechanisms, for example, when appeals made on a patient's behalf for medical or hospital care are arbitrarily ignored or unreasonably disregarded or overridden. However, the physician who complies without protest cannot avoid his ultimate responsibility for his patient's care. He cannot point to the health care payor as the liability scapegoat. (p. 819)

Although the physician was not sued in this instance, he was judged to be responsible for the outcome by failure to protest the utilization review company's decision.

In *Wilson* v. *Blue Cross*, a patient was admitted to a hospital for a major depressive episode, chemical dependency, and anorexia. The attending physician recommended three to four weeks of inpatient care. However, 10 days postadmission, the patient's insurance company, via an external utilization review company, denied payment for further care. This led to the patient's discharge. Three weeks later, he committed suicide.

The family sued Blue Cross and its utilization review company. They did not sue the physician. The insurance company argued that discharge was the responsibility of the attending physician. Based on the *Wickline* decision, the trial court agreed. The Court of Appeals, however, reversed this finding, indicating that there were triable issues as to whether the early discharge was a factor in the patient's death. The final adjudication of this case awaits the outcome on appeal.

Since these two cases are interlinked, and since both have received much media attention, a more extended discussion is in order. Wilson had insurance through a private policy from Blue Cross and Blue Shield of Alabama, providing for 30 days of inpatient mental health care per calendar year. When he moved to California, California Blue Cross assumed administration of the policy. Unlike the *Wickline* case, there was no clear or formalized appeals procedure, and the physician was uninformed that a right of appeal existed. This was a factor in the Court's remanding the case back to trial.

Although these two cases appear similar, they involve quite different causes of action. The *Wilson* case involved allegations of breach of contract; the *Wickline* case involved allegations of negligence. Since Wilson's Alabama insurance policy allowed 30 days of inpatient treatment, early discharge may have represented a breach of contract by the utilization review company. Additionally, since the attending physician recommended more inpatient care, utilization review may have corrupted his judgment. Again, the Court ruled that the ultimate responsibility for medical care belongs to the physician. The Appeals Court indicated that the link between the early discharge and the patient's subsequent suicide was a triable issue. If such a link is indeed determined, then the insurance company will be held liable.

In the *Wickline* case, unlike *Wilson*, utilization review was a known and well-established part of the insurance process. Furthermore, it was determined that medical standards of care were met in this case both by the attending physician and by the utilization review process. Finally, a formal appeals process was already in place, allowing the physician to challenge the decision of utilization review. Thus, in this case it was determined that the attending physician was responsible.

Although these cases are distinguishable, the barrier to liability for utilization review and third-party payers has been breached. This provides cause for concern to utilization review companies and to companies involved in managed medical care plans (including those covered under the Employee Retirement Income Security Act [ERISA] guidelines). Given these factors, an attorney engaged by the author made the following recommendations with regard to situations of this kind:

1. Sound medical/psychiatric judgment must rule over competing or corrupting influences. Treatment must meet community standards of practice, and accurate, complete documentation is the best way to determine that such care has indeed been rendered. As indicated, the physician bears ultimate responsibility for the patient's care. An appeal should be made in writing should the attending physician disagree with the decision from the utilization review.

2. It is important that managed care and utilization review companies provide formal review criteria that conform to the community standards of practice.

3. Whenever possible, the reviewer should actually see the patient rather than make a determination over the telephone.

4. It is also useful for the attending physician to obtain informed refusal from the patient, apprising him or her of the possible risks of treatment as well as the possible outcome should treatment fail to be obtained. The patient should also be informed of the costs in order help him or her to decide whether or not to pay for out-of-pocket treatment.

Suits such as those discussed in this chapter are inevitably painful for all involved, and proceedings can sometimes endure for years. As stated in preceding chapters, the use of capitation, while eliminating the perverse incentive of fee-for-service reimbursement, provides substitute incentive to deny appropriate care. With regard to managed mental health care, a significant deterrent to this policy, as demonstrated by *Wilson* v. *Blue Cross*, is the possibility of adverse outcome with attendant legal ramifications.

Chapter 10
Managed Mental Health Care Companies

Included in this chapter is a partial listing of managed mental health care companies with national (or large regional) presence. This information includes listings as well as partial descriptions of companies who responded to the author's letters of inquiry.

The location of detail about managed mental health care corporations is surprisingly difficult. There is as yet no separate business listing or reference manual for such companies. As a category, they are neither listed nor discussed by the American Managed Care Review Organization (AMCRA), the Group Health Association of America (GHAA), the American Psychiatric Association (APA), or the American Hospital Association (AHA). Contacts by the author with several managed companies indicated that they tend to have little "intelligence" about each other at the current time. The source listing in this chapter was obtained primarily through a listing of participants signing in at a national managed mental health care convention.

Given these constraints, the following information should be considered incomplete. Some companies with national presence may be missing from the source list. There are a number of other fine companies that, having a local or small regional presence only, may not be listed.

The accuracy of the "source descriptions" is probably quite good since information was in all cases provided by company representatives. (The author's letter of inquiry, however, was sent in June of 1991.) The material was primarily form (versus content) edited. The accuracy of the "content descriptions" is somewhat more suspect since information was obtained from third-party publications about companies (versus from company officials themselves). Finally, there is an alphabetical listing of the remaining managed mental health care companies for which address-only information was able to be obtained. Letters of inquiry went from the author to all companies included under the "content descriptions" and the general listings. Apparently, however, they were unable to respond.

The first source description is of MCC Managed Behavioral Care, Inc., the oldest and largest managed mental health care company in the country. Since the author worked for this company for nearly four years, the evaluations provided herein as to managed mental health care in general, and MCC in particular, may be considered a source of either valuable inside information or personal bias, depending upon perspective.

MCC management allowed the author 4 hours weekly of unpaid time from work, over a nine-month period, for the purpose of completing this book as well as an edited book on psychotherapy outcome (Giles, 1993). Other than in this capacity, they did not sponsor, condone, criticize, or interfere with this project in any way.

The author apologizes for any possible deletions from the list. In order to correct omissions for future editions of this book, company representatives may write to the following address:

Thomas R. Giles, Psy.D.
President
Associates in Managed Care
10200 East Girard Avenue
Suite C–356
Denver, Colorado 80231
(303)–337–9256
Fax: (303)–617–6312

Representatives wishing to provide company descriptions can use the original letter of inquiry, reprinted at the end of this chapter, as a guide.

Additional opinions about this book, managed mental health care, clinical psychology, and so forth (pro or con) will be welcomed. General correspondence of this sort can also be directed to the author at the address above.

SOURCE DESCRIPTIONS

The following descriptions are listed in order of decreasing magnitude of annual revenues and/or numbers of covered lives.

MCC Managed Behavioral Care, Inc.
11095 Viking Drive, Suite 350
Eden Prairie, Minnesota 55344
1-800-433-5768

Established in 1974 in Minneapolis, MCC was acquired by Cigna in January 1989. It has annual revenues of $120 million and responsibility for more than four million covered lives. The company is undergoing a period of substantial growth and is expected to double in the next two to three years.

Initial expansion occurred within HMO markets and emphasized capitated accounts. MCC is the managed mental health carrier for all Cigna insurance sites. It provides services for a number of other HMOs as well.

MCC will soon have a presence in almost all 50 states. Its mission statement indicates an interest in furthering its image as the leading managed mental health care company in the country. The company has a reputation for emphasis on quality of care.

MCC stresses a brief, empirically validated treatment approach for outpatient and inpatient case management. It has delineated criteria for the provision of outpatient care, inpatient case management, provider credentialing, utilization review, and customer service. It is a recognized leader in the efficient development of local networks tailored to meet a variety of business and clinical needs.

In recent years, MCC, in addition to HMO business, has placed emphasis on employer accounts. Depending on employer preferences, geographical location, schedule of needs, and a host of additional exigencies, MCC can provide case management and clinical services on a local and/or central basis. Access to central case management occurs through a toll-free number at a national service center, staffed 24 hours per day, 365 days per year with clinicians available for crisis assistance and immediate referral to provider networks. Services can generally be provided on a carve-out basis and paid for either through fee-for-service or capitation.

MCC has an extensive management information system (MIS) capable of tracking claims payment, provider efficiency, outpatient and inpatient utilization, and long-distance utilization review. Additional information can be obtained at the address or number listed above.

Health Risk Management
8000 West 78th Street
Minneapolis, MN 55439
(612) 829-3500

Mission Statement: To deliver excellent health care management services that will help our clients and their employees manage health care benefits in order to (1) reduce medically unnecessary, inappropriate, and/or harmful services; (2) improve quality; (3) promote good health; (4) control costs; and (5) to remain a profitable, growing, leading-edge, and internationally recognized health care management company.

Number of Covered Lives: 2,000,000

Revenues 1990: $17,088,00 (fiscal year ending June 30, 1990)

Number of Years in Business: 14 years (since 1977)

Geographic Area Served: Nationwide

Services: The following services are provided:

Inpatient Medical/Surgical	Total Back Management
Outpatient Medical/Surgical	Disability Management
Inpatient MH/CD	PPO
Outpatient MH/CD	Fee Negotiation and Bill
Pharmaceutical	Review
Outpatient Physical Therapy	EAP
Chiropractic	Benefit Analysis
Premature Birth Prevention	Claims Administration
Workers' Compensation	Communications

Achievement & Guidance Centers of America, Inc.
3 Friends Lane, Suite 200
Newtown, Pennsylvania 18940
(215) 579-2323; 1-800-800-2422
FAX: (215) 579-9920, 579-9921

Achievement & Guidance Centers of America, Inc. (AGCA) manages and provides mental health and substance abuse programs utilizing its own staff and independent professional providers. The objective of AGCA's programs is to deliver quality mental health care, to increase the effectiveness in delivering the care, and to manage the costs of such care under health benefit plans sponsored by its clients. AGCA has adapted and enhanced general managed health care techniques to effectively address the delivery systems, cost structures, and utilization characteristics of mental health care.

AGCA offers to its clients, on a capitated-fee basis, a comprehensive managed mental health program that integrates patient evaluation, referral to the company's staff providers or independent provider network, and concurrent utilization review. AGCA also contracts to provide utilization review and claims administration separately. As part of the company's programs, networks are established with psychiatrists, psychologists, social workers, and health care facilities. These health care providers agree to provide services at discounted rates and abide by plan rules relating to matters such as utilization review, quality assurance, and professional licensing. The company's utilization review and case management procedures are applied with its staff providers and provider networks to give customers an integrated cost-containment solution to mental health care needs.

The company markets its programs in major metropolitan areas to health maintenance organizations, insurance companies, employers, unions, and the public sector. As of March 31, 1991, AGCA services benefit plans that cover approximately 1.4 million persons of 19 clients, including U.S. Healthcare, Aetna Life and Casualty Company ("Aetna"), New York Life Insurance Company ("N.Y. Life"), and The Travelers Companies ("Travelers").

Care is delivered either through the company's providers at the staff offices or through the independent provider network. Currently, there are 12 staff offices located in the Delaware Valley and six located at the AGCA regional offices in Chapel Hill, North Carolina; Dallas, Texas; Manchester, New Hampshire; Newtown, Pennsylvania; New York City; and Washington, DC. AGCA has established a provider network in 22 markets located in 14 states, which is comprised of approximately 3,500 practitioners and 117 facilities.

These practitioners and facilities must meet AGCA's clinical review standards and provide services at prenegotiated rates to beneficiaries of health plans offered by the company's clients. The majority of AGCA's contracts are based on a capitated rate known as a per-member, per-month fee. Together with its clients, AGCA analyzes the client's historical cost and utilization data for psychiatric and substance abuse treatment and designs a customized benefit plan that attempts to balance plan benefits with cost. AGCA receives a fixed premium per plan beneficiary and is responsible for paying all approved claims, thereby assuming the risk that claims may exceed premiums paid.

Background and Strategy. AGCA was formed in 1982 by Steven Picow and Arthur Katz, who recognized the potential business opportunity for managing the costs and delivery of mental health care. AGCA's strategy has been to develop and introduce specialized managed mental health programs with the objective of promoting better access to cost-effective outpatient care while better managing the cost and quality of any required inpatient care. Picow and Katz, along with two psychologists, Dr. Lawrence Decker and Dr. Howard Savin, obtained AGCA's first client, U.S. Healthcare, in 1982.

Over the last 10 years, the company has developed a proprietary set of management techniques for mental health care, referred to as the Systems Approach. The core of AGCA's Systems Approach is the development of a continuum of managed health care that helps to ensure accountability and cost control of quality health care. The Systems Approach offers (1) customized plans designed to achieve each client's cost and benefit objectives; (2) access to the company's staff providers and preferred provider networks comprising both practitioners and facilities; (3) telephone-based patient evaluation, referral, and concurrent review by professional clinicians; and (4) claims review and management reporting and analysis.

The Systems Approach relies on the blending of aggressive contracting with providers of care, rigorous inpatient utilization management, and careful treatment review. Treatment review is the process of the assessment and selection of the appropriate level of care by AGCA employees. Access to outpatient care is enhanced through the AGCA treatment review process and costly inpatient care is controlled.

Benefit Plan Design and Pricing. AGCA and each of its clients jointly analyze the client's historical cost and utilization data for psychiatric and substance abuse treatment and design a customized benefit plan that attempts to balance plan benefits with cost. AGCA receives a fixed premium per plan beneficiary and is responsible for paying all approved claims, thereby assuming the risk that claims may exceed premiums paid. AGCA's per-member, per-month (pmpm) fee ranges from $1.70 to $6.00 per covered life. This rate will vary based on utilization history of the client and amount of options in the benefit package. The majority of physicians are compensated on a fee-for-service basis, although some receive capitated rates. AGCA is one of the most cost-competitive companies in the industry. In many cases price is the deciding factor in awarding contracts.

Staff Models and Provider Networks. Upon entering a new market, AGCA establishes a network of providers. If the market becomes large enough (50,000 or more covered lives) the company will consider developing a staff model facility, which is a facility where the providers are employees of the company rather than independent contractors. A clinical director is located at each staff office to review the patient cases. Although the staff model is more expensive to operate than a network of providers (because of additional overhead expenses), it is often more profitable due to the company's ability to monitor the delivered care. In the Delaware Valley, most patients receive care through the company's staff model offices. In other markets, care is presently delivered approximately 5 percent through staff model offices and 95 percent through the provider network. AGCA intends to increase the number of staff offices so that approximately 50 percent of the care is provided through staff offices. Staff offices have approximately 200 appointments per week and an 8-to-14-member staff.

AGCA has developed provider networks for mental health and substance abuse care in major metropolitan areas. These practitioners and facilities must meet AGCA's clinical review standards and provide services at prenegotiated rates to beneficiaries of health plans offered by the company's clients. Treatment responsibilities rest solely with the network providers to whom beneficiaries are referred.

The company's provider network typically includes inpatient acute care providers, residential chronic care and/or transitional care providers, and individual, group, or clinical outpatient providers of psychiatric or substance abuse treatment. The number and type of providers in a particular network depend upon the size and geographic concentration of the beneficiary population the network is intended to serve, and the population's historical and expected utilization patters. AGCA has established eligibility criteria for inclusion in a network and monitors network providers based on such criteria on an ongoing basis.

For a practitioner, these eligibility criteria cover proper licensing, clinical experience, and the need for the practitioner's specialty in the network. Providers generally enter into one-year, automatically renewable, contracts that require the maintenance of good professional standing and compliance with the company's quality, utilization, and administrative guidelines and procedures.

As of March 32, 1991, AGCA had established provider networks in 22 markets located in 14 states, comprised of approximately 3,500 practitioners and 117 facilities. In addition, AGCA operates 18 staff model facilities, with 13 located in the Delaware Valley and 5 located at the company's regional offices, with approximately 100 providers.

Utilization Management and Quality Assurance. At AGCA the clinical and administrative staff work in concert to provide timely reviews of clinical services and standards of care. The Corporate Quality Assurance Committee oversees an ongoing process by which selected clinical monitors are reviewed and criteria are established. In doing so, a conduit for communication is created to assure that refinements in care are sustained. In addition, information derived from the monitoring and evaluation activities are shared with other services and merged as appropriate with information obtained throughout the organization.

AGCA recognizes that quality and the degree of adherence to accepted clinical principles are reflective to contemporary standards of good practice. The Committee strives to assess that efficient, but not excessive, use of a particular procedure or treatment or service is provided and that the setting in which the treatments are offered are best suited to meet the patient's needs. The Quality Assurance Committee maintains a fluid and dynamic approach to quality standards, monitoring and developing criteria through a review of contemporary literature, examination of standards of care within a professional practice, as well as among standards already set by AGCA's Policy and Procedures. While no specific number of criteria is selected, the criteria selected do relate specifically to the indicator and do distinguish between acceptable and unacceptable levels of care.

The Utilization Management Program, a component of the Corporate Quality Assurance Activities, is a process by which patient care is reviewed to determine if the services provided are clinically necessary and if they are being provided in the most appropriate clinical setting. A portion of this program is conducted by Utilization Review Coordinators for both independent and delegated review. Special problems or cases are reviewed at the request of the Corporate Quality Assurance Committee. These reviews are used as a basis for reviewing provider practice patterns with respect to a variety of parameters, including diagnosis, level of care, length of care, and discharge planning activities. Inpatient utilization review staff work toward the effective and appropriate discharge of the patient from the time of entry into a treatment facility. Emphasis is on the development of the comprehensive aftercare network; therefore, active planning of the patient's treatment in the least restrictive environment is a goal of the department. The department strives to monitor the needed services and to have the case returned to the community and preexisting social network at the earliest possible time.

AGCA also provides a forum by which participating facilities and providers may appeal decisions regarding their utilization of the patient's benefit or a specific question regarding the utilization of services. It provides an opportunity to the participating facilities to appeal internal decisions regarding a patient's treatment programs in an objective manner, for reconsideration or revision of AGCA's administrative and clinical recommendations. While these appeals and reviews are performed in-house, AGCA maintains an affiliation with a nationally known review organization, for "third-level" independent medical review.

CMG Health
Corporate Offices
25 Crossroads Drive
Owing Mills, Maryland 21117
(301) 581-5000; 1-800-777-7753

CMG provides services through three basic behavioral health programs. These programs are configured to help solve today's problems with respect to mental health and chemical dependency in the workplace and in the family.

Comprehensive Managed Mental Health and Chemical Dependency Programs include 24-hour access and triage, precertification, patient referral to clinicians, concurrent review, case management, discharge planning, retrospective review, and claims processing and payment.

Utilization Management Programs include precertification, concurrent review, referral to network, and varying levels of case management.

Employee Assistance Programs (EAPs) include assessment, problem solving, and/or referral services for employees who need assistance with mental health and/or chemical dependency problems. EAPs can be an entry point into the CMG system and a source of ongoing services.

CMG's operating principles include (1) valuing quality patient care, (2) providing easily accessible care, (3) stressing communication, and (4) applying total quality management.

Emphasis on the patient stems from CMG's inception as a company founded by clinicians who know the importance of timely and appropriate care. CMG also recognizes the patient's need for easily accessible care. Thus, caregivers are not only the best in their field but they provide a broad range of clinical specialties available at convenient locations.

Whether interacting with patients, clinicians, or payers, CMG insists on clear communication. It is an imperative at CMG and it is what helps to make the company so efficient and effective in providing behavioral health managed care arrangements that respect both quality care and cost-contained care.

CMG sets standards for management and patient care and constantly monitors both through a process called Total Quality Management. The never-ending cycle of checks keeps CMG focused on quality care and cost containment. It also reassures clients that the company enforces its own expectation to continually improve behavioral healthcare.

At the heart of CMG Health's managed care approach is the insistence on maintaining quality patient care. The company believes that managed care means improving care while containing costs. CMG was established in 1985 to work with insurers, employers, HMOs, PPOs, and third-party administrators in providing effective behavioral health care through managed care arrangements. It is a national firm working closely with patients, families, attending physicians, and clients in a collaborative effort aimed at accessible and medically appropriate care.

CMG develops and implements its flexible programs primarily in response to client needs. Regardless of what services a client requires, the staff constantly monitors and documents all activities so that the staff can report to clients in a timely and accurate way. CMG's proprietary management information system enables the company to be highly efficient. Its focus on appropriate and timely treatment, and its dedication to a process called Total Quality Management distinguishes CMG in the managed behavioral health care field.

American Mental Health Care, Inc.
4730 North Habana Avenue, Suite 202
Tampa, Florida 33614
(813) 874-0849; 1-800-330-3816

American Mental Health Care, Inc. (AMHC) is a Florida-based corporation established in 1986 that provides nationwide mental health and chemical dependency case management and treatment services and EAP services for employers, HMOs, PPOs, the insurance industry, and other management care companies. At this time, discounted networks are available only in Florida and a few additional sites in the southeast.

The managed mental health care system developed by AMHC in Florida is a comprehensive acute care system characterized by an emphasis on accessibility, quality of care, and multiple levels of care that enable patients to be treated in the most cost-effective manner. Consistent with extensive research data, the AMHC system conceptualizes optimal treatment as the level of treatment that meets the patients' needs while minimally interrupting their normal lives.

AMHC's approach to managed mental health services is based on the principal that enrollees should receive all of the care that they legitimately need, but no more than they need. Excessive care, or care of an unnecessary level of intensity, is perceived as a disservice to a patient's self-esteem, coping abilities, and likelihood of future success. Care that builds on a patient's abilities and high expectations for successful outcome results in briefer periods of disablement and an enhanced likelihood of successful coping during future stressful periods. Nontraditional and/or outpatient treatment modalities utilized by MAHC are firmly based on available research results.

In addition to providing the best mental health treatment and case management services for employees and HMO/PPO enrollees, AMHC consciously endeavors to generate a cost savings on general medical services costs through intensive treatment of mental health patients who appear to be overutilizing or inappropriately utilizing general medical services.

AMC provides directly all case management services, including EAP, triage, and utilization review for managed care enrollees. Direct treatment services are provided by an extensive network of excellent providers who have contracted with AMHC to provide services at significant discounts. Only licensed outpatient therapists are utilized. Therapists available include psychiatrists, psychologists, MSW's, occupational therapists, nurses, and Certified Additions Treatment specialists. Only JCAHO-certified facilities are used for inpatient care.

All care provided is managed care and is provided under the supervision of a physician. In practice, AMHC provides a system of care that closely approximates a staff-model HMO for mental health services.

AMHC can provide all levels of managed mental health care services, from simple second opinions, to EAP services, to full-risk capitated services. The company will custom design a program that includes all of the specific elements desired by an employer or prepaid health plan. Although AMHC is clearly striving to provide the very best managed mental health care services, its charges are usually very competitive, sometimes lower than those of competitors who provide considerably less service. The AMHC emphasis on keeping enrollees productive, generating a cost offset in general medical care, and providing the most cost-effective mental health services maximizes the cost savings to purchasers.

Behavioral Health Resources
3752 Elizabeth Street
Riverside, California 92506
(714) 275-8600

BHR has been in existence since 1987 and currently manages over 400,000 lives in a six-county southern California area. Its mission statement is to assure that the appropriate level of care is provided to the patients based on their individual needs and the health benefits they have. Clients range from at-risk, carve-out arrangements with HMOs and Independent Practice Associations (IPAs) to management fee contracts with CHAMPUS Reform Initiative Activities (Prime and Extra programs).

BHR's Managed Care Division provides the following services: (1) an entirely telephone-based case management system, (2) a daily medical director who reviews all denials, (3) a sophisticated computer system that supports case management and provides specific utilization data, (4) six county southern California Provider Network, (5) fully integrated Employee Assistance and Managed Care Services, and (6) total claims adjudication and payment capabilities.

HMA Behavioral Health, Inc.
255 Park Avenue
Worcester, Massachusetts 01609
(508) 757-2290; 1-800-248-9908
FAX: (508) 754-3616

HMA Behavioral Health, Inc. was founded in 1982 to provide mental health and substance abuse services to prepaid health insurance plans and other group purchasers of health care. The company began with a small HMO in central Massachusetts servicing 14,000 lives. Today it services approximately 300,000 lives throughout Massachusetts, Maine, and Connecticut. Revenues are in excess of $4.5 million.

HMA embraces a philosophy of timely, responsive, high-quality and humane patient care. Care and management networks are built on that foundation, selecting only those providers who subscribe to that philosophy. The company believes that treatment programs that are medically necessary and therapeutically appropriate are indeed cost-effective. HMA does not advocate reduced benefits or restricted services. As it was in 1982, HMA's mission today is to attain the efficient delivery of mental health and substance abuse services while maintaining and enhancing high-quality care.

The bulk of HMA's business is in the New England states. Its customer base consists of IPA model HMOs and self-insured companies. Services include full-risk carve-outs, managed PPOs, utilization management, and EAP services.

HMA prefers to collaborate with community providers. It is not HMA's preference to displace community providers with separate clinics, rather the company seeks to utilize the local providers and to integrate the existing resources into an efficient delivery system. In terms of system design, HMA prefers triage sites for chemical dependency. For mental health, HMA recommends an open access system. Its preferred financial arrangement is full-risk capitation.

CONTENT DESCRIPTIONS

The following companies are listed in alphabetical order. The primary source for this information was the January 14, 1991, issue of *Healthweek*.

American Biodyne, Inc.
400 Oyster Point Boulevard, #306
San Francisco, California 94080

This company covers more than 2 million lives. It was founded in 1985 by Albert Waxman, who also founded several multimillion dollar medical/electronic products companies. One of Biodyne's major markets is in Illinois, where 400,000 lives are under coverage.

American Psychmanagement
1560 Wilson Boulevard, Suite 1000
Arlington, Virginia 22209

This company covers more than 3 million lives with its utilization review, case management, and PPO network contracts. It is owned by Valuehealth of Avon, Connecticut. This company currently holds the IBM contract and is assembling a network of up to 12,000 providers to serve IBM's 700,000 employees, dependents, and retirees.

Human Affairs International
5801 South Fashion Boulevard
Murray, Utah 84107

Some 3.3 million covered lives are this company's responsibility. It specializes in managed mental health care and is owned by Aetna Life Insurance Company of Hartford, Connecticut.

Managed Health Network
5100 West Goldleaf Circle, #300
Los Angeles, California 90056

This company covers nearly 2 million employees and dependents. It is a possible buyout target of Metropolitan Life. It currently has $31 million in annual revenues and 270 employees.

Preferred Health Care Ltd.
P.O. Box 787
Welton, Conneticut 06897

This is the only publicly traded managed mental health care firm. It covers 1.2 million lives and markets its services as PsychCare. Revenues exceeded $35 million in 1991.

United Behavioral Systems, Inc.
3600 West 80th Street, #210
Minneapolis, Minnesota 55431

This company covers about 1 million lives through its clinical services program and another 1 million lives through utilization review and case management services. It is owned by United Health Care Corporation of Minnetonka, Minnesota.

U.S. Behavioral Health
2000 Powell, #1180
Emerville, California 94608

This company is owned by Traveler's Corporation of Hartford, Connecticut. It covers more than 4 million members and manages 90 provider networks around the country.

GENERAL LISTINGS

Behavioral Health, Inc.
143 Ridgeway, #118
Lafayette, Louisiana 70503

Behavioral Health Resources
3752 Elizabeth Street
Riverside, California 92506

Health Risk Management
8000 West 78th Street
Minneapolis, Minnesota 55439

Interpsych Associates
700 South Henderson Road, #230B
King of Prussia, Pennsylvania 19406

United Health Plan
18531 Roscoe Boulevard
Northridge, California 91325

SAMPLE LETTER OF INQUIRY

Dear _____ :

I am writing to request that you provide me with information about your managed mental health care company. The information will be used to help prospective buyers of managed mental health care services access your company for further information, consultation, and RFPs. I will arrange to print this material, with only minimal editing, in the concluding chapter in my forthcoming book, *Managed Mental Health Care: A Guide for Practitioners, Employers, and Hospital Administrators,* published by Allyn and Bacon.

Please disclose as much or as little about your company as you feel is appropriate. Such information might include company name, address, and phone number; names and titles of top management; number of covered lives; annual revenues; number of years in business; mission statement; philosophy of inpatient and outpatient mental health/substance abuse treatment; geographical availability; customer base/services (EAP, EPO, ASO, capitation, discounted fee-for-service, claims payments); and a general description of the company's preferred methods of operation.

The book provides a general explication of managed mental health care services, describing them in a balanced but generally favorable light. It does not favor one company over another.

Should you find this request of interest, please provide 1–4 pages of information, double spaced.

I hope that my book will provide referral business to your fine company.

Sincerely,

Thomas R. Giles, Psy.D.
Executive Director
MCC of Colorado

References

Aiken, L., & Marx, M. (1982). Hospices: Perspectives on the national policy debate. *American Psychologist, 37,* 1271-1279.

Alexander, J., & Parsons, J.(1973). Short-term behavioral intervention with delinquent families. *Journal of Abnormal Psychology, 81,* 219-225.

American Medical Care Review Association (AMCRA). (1986). *Directory of preferred provider organizations and the industry report on PPO development.* Bethesda, MD: Author.

American Psychological Association. (1990). Ethical principles of psychologists (amended June 2, 1989). *American Psychologist, 45,* 390-395.

Amler, R., & Duhl, L. (1984). *Closing the gap.* Oxford: Oxford Press.

Andrews, G., & Harvey, R. (1981). Does psychotherapy benefit neurotic patients? *Archives of General Psychiatry, 38,* 1203-1208.

Armenti, N. (1991). The provider network in managed care. *Behavior Therapist, 14,* 123-128.

Ascher, L. M. (1981). Employing paradoxical intention in the treatment of agoraphobia. *Behavior Research and Therapy, 19,* 110.

Ascher, L. M. & Turner, R. (1980). A comparison of the two methods for the administration of paradoxical intention. *Behavior Research and Therapy, 18,* 121-126.

Azrin, N. (1976) Improvements in the community-reinforcement approach to alcoholism. *Behavior Research and Therapy, 14,* 339-348.

Azrin, N., Nunn, R., & Frantz, S. (1979). Comparison of regulated breathing versus abbreviated desensitization on reported stuttering episodes. *Journal of Speech and Hearing Disorders, 44,* 331-339.

Azrin, N. Nunn, R., & Frantz, S. (1980). Habit reversal vs. Negative practice treatment of nervous tics. *Behavior Therapy, 2,* 169-178.

Balinger, J. (1990, January). *Pharmacotherapy of panic disorders.* International Conference on Panic Disorders, Gothenberg, Sweden.

Barlow, D., & Cerny, J. (1988). *Psychological treatment of panic.* New York: Guilford.

Barlow, D., Leitenberg, H., & Agras, W. (1969). Experimental control of sexual deviation through manipulation of the noxious scene in covert sensitization. *Journal of Abnormal Psychology, 74,* 596-601.

Beauchamp, T., & Childress, W. (1988). *Principles of biomedical ethics* (3rd ed.). Baltimore, MD: Johns Hopkins University Press.

Beck, A. (1991). Cognitive therapy: A 30-year retrospective. *American Psychologist, 46,* 369–375.

Beck, A., Rush, A., Shaw, B., & Emery, G. (1979). *Cognitive therapy of depression.* New York: Guilford.

Bellack, A., Hersen, J., & Himmelhoch, J. (1983). A comparison of social skills training, pharmacotherapy, and psychotherapy for depression. *Behavior Research and Therapy, 21,* 101–107.

Bellack, A., Turner, S., Hersen, M., & Luber, R. (1984). An examination of the efficacy of social skills training for schizophrenic patients. *Hospital and Community Psychiatry, 35,* 1023–1028.

Biran, M., & Wilson, G. (1980). *Participant modeling versus cognitive restructuring in the treatment of phobic disorders.* Association for the Advancement of Behavior Therapy, New York.

Bittker, T. (185). The industrialization of American psychiatry. *American Journal of Psychiatry, 142,* 149–154.

Blake, D., Abueg, F., Woodward, S., & Keane, T. (1993). Post-traumatic stress disorder: Comparative research. In T. Giles (Ed.), *Handbook of effective psychotherapy.* New York: Plenum.

Borkovec, T., & Mathews, A. (1988) Treatment of nonphobic anxiety disorder's: A comparison of nondirective, cognitive, and coping desensitization therapy. *Journal of Consulting and Clinical Psychology, 56,* 877–884.

Borkovec, T., Mathews, A., Chambers, A., Ebrahami, S., Lytle, R., & Nelson, R. (1987). The effects of relaxation training with cognitive or nondirective therapy and the role of relaxation-induced anxiety in the treatment of generalized anxiety. *Journal of Consulting and Clinical Psychology, 55,* 883–888.

Bornstein, P. (1981). *Behavioral-communications treatment of marital discord.* Association for the Advancement of Behavior Therapy, Toronto.

Brace, N. (1990, November). Contracting with managed care plans: Survival techniques. *Colorado Psychology Association Bulletin,* 1–6.

Braun, P., Kochansky, U., Shapiro, R., Greenberg, S., Gudeman, J., Johnson, S., & Shore, M. (1981). Overview: Deinstitutionalization of psychiatric patients, a critical review of outcome studies. *American Journal of Psychiatry, 138,* 736–749.

Brook, B. (1973). An alternative to hospitalization for emergency patients. *Hospital and Community psychiatry, 24,* 621–624.

Brownell, K., & Wadden, T. (1991). The heterogeneity of obesity: Fitting treatments to individuals. *Behavior Therapy, 22,* 153–178.

Butler, G., Fennell, M., Robson, P., & Gelder, M. (1991). Comparison of behavior therapy and cognitive behavior therapy in the treatment of generalized anxiety disorder. *Journal of Consulting and Clinical Psychology, 59,* 167–175.

Califano, A. (1986). A corporate Rx for America: Managing runaway health cost. *Issues in Science and Technology, 2,* 81–90.

Casey, R., & Berman, J. (1985). The outcome of psychotherapy with children. *Psychological Bulletin, 98,* 388–400.

Cioffi, F. (1960). Freud and the idea of a pseudo-science. In R. Boryer and F. Cioffi (Eds.), *Explanation in the behavioral sciences*. Cambridge: Cambridge University Press.

Clum, G. (1989). Psychological interventions vs. drugs in the treatment of panic. *Behavior therapy, 20,* 429–458.

Cooper, N., & Clum, G. (1989). Imaginal flooding as a supplementary treatment for PTSD in combat veterans: A controlled study. *Behavior Therapy, 20,* 381–391.

Cooper, R. (1989). Employer's view of managed health care. In P. Kongstvedt (Ed.), *The managed health care handbook*. Rockville, MD: Aspen.

Cooper, J., Gelder, M., & Marks, I. (1965). Results of behavior therapy with 77 psychiatric patients. *British Medical Journal, 1,* 1222–1225.

Covi, L., & Lipman, R. (1987). Cognitive-behavioral group psychotherapy combined with imipramine in major depression. *Psychopharmacological Bulletin, 23,* 173–176.

Covi, L., Lipman, R., Derogatis, L., Smith, J., & Pattison, J. (1974). Drugs and group psychotherapy in neurotic depression. *American Journal of Psychiatry, 131,* 191–198.

Craighead, L., & Agras, S. (1991). Mechanisms of action in cognitive behavioral and pharmacological interventions for obesity and bulimia nervosa. *Journal of Consulting and Clinical Psychology, 59,* 115–125.

Cummings, N. (1987). The future of psychotherapy: One psychologist's perspective. *American Journal of Psychotherapy, 61,* 349–360.

Cummins, N., & Duhl, L. (1986). The new delivery system. *Psychiatric Annals, 16,* 470–475.

Davies, N., & Felder, L. (1990). Applying brakes to the runaway American health care system. *Journal of the American Medical Association, 263,* 73–76.

Davis, A., Dinitz, S., & Pasamanick, B. (1972). The prevention of hospitalization in schizophrenia: Five years after an experimental program. *American Journal of Orthopsychiatry, 43,* 375–388.

Davis, K., Anderson, G., Rowland, D., & Steinberg, E. (1990). *Health care cost containment*. Baltimore: Johns Hopkins University Press.

Deming, E. (1988). *Out of the crisis*. Boston: Massachusetts Institute of Technology Press.

Dobson, K. (1989). A meta analysis of the efficacy of cognitive therapy for depression. *Journal of Consultive and Clinical Psychology, 57,* 414–419.

DeRubeis, R., & Hollon, S. (1981). Behavioral treatment of affective disorders. In M. Hersen & S. Turner (Eds.), *Future perspectives in behavior therapy*. New York: Plenum.

de Shazer, D. (1985). *Keys to solution in brief therapy*. New York: Norton.

Durham, R., & Turvey, A. (1987). Cognitive therapy vs. behavior therapy in the treatment of chronic general anxiety. *Behavior Research and Therapy, 25,* 229–234.

Dworkin, S., & Kerr, B. (1987). Comparison of interventions for women experiencing body image problems. *Journal of Consulting and Clinical Psychology, 34,* 136–140.

Eisler, R. & Hersen, M. (1973). *The A-B design: Effects of token economy on behavioral and subjective measures in neurotic depression.* American Psychological Association, Montreal, Canada.

Elkin, I., Parloff, J., Hadley, S., & Autry, J. (1985). NIMH treatment of depression collaborative research program. *Archives of General Psychiatry, 42,* 305–316.

English, J., Sharfstein, S., Scherl, D., Astrachan, B., & Muszynski, I. (1986.). Diagnosis-related groups and general hospital psychiatry: The APA study. *American Journal of Psychiatry, 143,* 131–139.

Fairburn, C., Kirk, J., O'Connor, M., & Cooper, P. (1986). A comparison of two psychological treatments for bulimia nervosa. *Behavior Research and Therapy, 24,* 629–643.

Falloon, I., McGill, C., Boyd, J., & Pederson, J. (1987). Family management in the prevention of morbidity of schizophrenia: Social outcome of a two-year longitudinal study. *Psychological Medicine, 17,* 59–66.

Falloon, I., & Pederson, J. (1985). Family management in the prevention of morbidity in schizophrenia: The adjustment of the family. *British Journal of Psychiatry, 147,* 156–163.

Feinsilver, D. (1983). Application of Pao's theories to a case study of the use and misuse of medication. *Psychoanalytic Inquiry, 3,* 125–144.

Feinsilver, D. (1986). *Towards a comprehensive model of schizophrenic disorders: Psychoanalytic essays in memory of Ping-Nie Pao.* Hillsdale, NJ: Analytic Press.

Flinn, D., McMahon, T., & Collins, M. (1987). Health maintenance organizations and their implications to psychiatry. *Hospital and Community Psychiatry, 38,* 255–262.

Flomenhaft, K., Kaplan, D., & Langsley, D. (1969). Avoiding psychiatric hospitalization. *Social Work, 16,* 38–45.

Foa, E., Jameson, J., Turner, R., & Payne, L. (1980). Massed vs. spaced exposure sessions in the treatment of agoraphobia. *Behavior research and Therapy, 18,* 33–338.

Foa, E., Steketee, G., & Milby, J. (1980). Differential effects of exposure and response prevention in obsessive-compulsive washers. *Journal of Consulting and Clinical Psychology, 48,* 71–79.

Forgatch, M., & Patterson, G. (1989). *Living together, Part 2: Family problem solving.* Eugene, OR: Castalia.

Foster Higgins & Co (1989). *Mental health and substance avenues benefits survey.* Princeton, NJ: Author.

Friedman, A. (1975). Interaction of drug therapy with marital therapy in depressed patients. *Archives of General Psychiatry, 32,* 619–637.

Gallagher, D., & Thompson, L. (1982). Treatment of major depressive disorder in older adult outpatients with brief psychotherapies. *Psychotherapy: Theory, research, and practice, 19,* 482–490.

Garfield, S. (1980). *Psychotherapy: An eclectic approach.* New York: Wiley.

Garfield, S. (1989) *The practice of brief psychotherapy.* New York: Pergamon.

Gelder, M., Bancroft, J., Gath, D., Johnston, D., Mathews, A., & Shaw, P. (1973). Specific and nonspecific factors in behavior therapy. *British Journal of Psychiatry, 123,* 445–462.

Gelder, M., and Marks, I. (1968). A crossover study of desensitization in phobias. *British Journal of Psychiatry, 114,* 323–328.

Gelder, M., & Marks, I., & Wolff, H. (1967). Desensitization and psychotherapy in the treatment of phobic states: A controlled inquiry. *British Journal of Psychiatry, 113,* 53–73.

Giles, T. (1983a). Probable superiority of behavioral interventions—I: Traditional comparative outcome. *Journal of Behavior Therapy and Experimental Psychiatry, 14,* 29–32.

Giles, T. (1983b). Probable superiority of behavioral interventions—II: Some implications for the ethical practice of psychological therapy. *Journal of Behavior Therapy and Experimental Psychiatry, 14,* 189–196.

Giles, T. (1984). Probable superiority of behavioral interventions—III: Some obstacles to acceptance of findings. *Journal of Behavior Therapy and Experimental Psychiatry, 15,* 23–26.

Giles, T. (1989). *Ethical considerations in managed mental health care systems.* American Psychological Association Convention, New Orleans.

Giles, T. (1990a). Bias against behavior therapy in outcome reviews: Who speaks for the patient? *Behavior Therapist, 19,* 86–90.

Giles, T. (1990b). Underutilization of effective psychotherapy: Managed mental health care and other forces of change. *Behavior Therapist, 19,* 107–110.

Giles, T. (1990c). *Managed mental health care: Treatment of complex cases.* Office of the Governor, Communities For a Drug Free Colorado, Denver, CO.

Giles, T. (1991). *Interface of managed mental health care and the private practice of psychology.* Colorado Psychological Association, Denver, CO.

Giles, T. (Ed.) (1993). *Handbook of effective Psychotherapy.* New York: Plenum.

Giles, T. (in press). Managed mental health care and effective psychotherapy: A step in the right direction? *Journal of Behavior Therapy and Experimental Psychiatry.*

Giles, T., & Hom, P. (1987). *New evidence on the comparative effectiveness of behavior therapy.* Presented at the Annual Meeting of the Association for the Advancement of Behavior Therapy, Boston, MA.

Giles, T., Prial, L., & Neims, D. (1993). Equivalence revisited: Directive psychotherapies. in T. Giles (Ed.), *Handbook of effective psychotherapy.* New York: Plenum.

Giles, T., Young, R., & Young, D. (1985). Behavioral treatment of severe bulimia. *Behavior Therapy, 19,* 101–111.

Gillan, P., & Rachman, S. (1974). An experimental investigation of behavior therapy in phobic patients. *British Journal of Psychiatry, 124,* 392–401.

Glover, E. (1959). Critical notice. *British Journal of Medical Psychology, 39,* 68–74.

Goffman, E. (1961). *Essays on the social situation of mental patients and other inmates.* Garden City, NY: Doubleday.

Goldman, H., & Taube, C. (1988). High users of outpatient mental health services. II: Implications for practice and policy. *American Journal of Psychiatry, 145,* 24–28.

Goldstein, M. (1979). The sociology of mental health and illness. *Annual Review of Sociology, 5,* 381–409.

Group Health Association of America (GHAA). (1988). *HMO industry Profile: Financial performance*. Washington, DC: Author.

Gudeman, J., Dickey, B., Evans, A., & Shore, M. (1985). Four-year assessment of a day hospital-inn program as an alternative to inpatient hospitalization. *American Journal of Psychiatry, 142*, 1330–1333.

Gunderson, J., Frank, A., Katz, H., Vannicelli, M., Frosch, J., & Knapp, P. (1984). Effects of psychotherapy in schizophrenia: II. Comparative outcome of two forms of treatment. *Schizophrenia Bulletin, 10*, 564–598.

Haas, L., & Cummings, N. (1991). Managed outpatient mental health plans: Clinical, ethical, and practical guidelines for participation. *Professional Psychology: Research and Practice, 22*, 45–51.

Haley, J. (1963). *Strategies of psychotherapy*. New York: Brune and Stratton.

Haley, J. (1973). *Uncommon therapy*. New York: Norton.

Hartlage, L. (1970). Subprofessional therapists' use of reinforcement versus traditional psychotherapeutic techniques with schizophrenics. *Journal of Consulting and Clinical Psychology, 34*, 181–183.

Hayashida, M., Alterman, A., McClellan, T., O'Brien, L., Purtill, B., Volpicelli, J., Raphaelson, A., & Hall, C. (1989). Comparative effectiveness and costs of inpatient and outpatient detoxification of patients with mid-to-moderate alcohol withdrawal syndrome. *New England Journal of Medicine, 320*, 358–365.

Hayes, S. (1987). Bracing for change. *Behavior Analysis, 32*, 710.

Herman, S., Barlow, D., & Agras, W. (1974). An experimental analysis of classical conditioning as a method of increasing heterosexual arousal in homosexuals. *Behavior Therapy, 5*, 33–47.

Hogarty, G., Anderson, C., Reiss, D., Kornblith, S., Greenwald, D., Jauna, C., & Madonia, M. (1986). Family psychoeducation, social skills training and medication in schizophrenia: I. One year effects of a controlled study on relapse and expressed emotion. *Archives of General Psychiatry, 43*, 633–642.

Holder, H. (1987). Alcoholism treatment and potential health care cost savings. *Medical Care*, 53–71.

Holder, H., & Blose, J. (1987). Changes in health care costs and utilization associated with mental health treatment. *Hospital and Community Psychiatry, 38*, 1070–1075.

Hollon, S., & Najavits, L. (1988). Review of empirical studies of cognitive therapy. In A. Frances & R. Hales (Eds.) *American Psychiatric Press Review of Psychiatry* (Vol. 7). Washington, DC: American Psychiatric Press.

Hollon, S., Shelton, R., & Loosen, P. (1991). Cognitive therapy and pharmacotherapy for depression. *Journal of Consulting and Clinical Psychology, 59*, 88–99.

Holt, R. (1965). A review of some of Freud's biological assumptions and their influence on his theories. In N. Grenfield & W. Lewis (Eds.), *Psychoanalysis and current biological thought*. Madison: University of Wisconsin Press.

Ingelhart, J. (1985). Medicare turns to HMOs. *New England Journal of Medicine, 312*, 132–136.

Jacobson, N. (1977). Training couples to solve their marital problems. *International Journal of Family Counsel, 4*, 22–31.

Jacobson, N. (1978). Specific and non-specific factors in the effectiveness of a behavioral approach to the treatment of marital discord. *Journal of Consulting and Clinical Psychology, 46,* 442–452.

Jansen, M. (1986). Emotional disorders and the labor force. *International Labor Review, 125,* 605–615.

Johnson, S., & Greenberg, L. (1985). Differential effects of experiential and problem-solving interventions in resolving marital conflict. *Journal of Consulting and Clinical Psychology, 53,* 175–184.

Jones, K., & Vischi, T. (1979). Impact of alcohol, drug abuse and mental health treatment on medical Care utilization. *Medical care, 17* (December Supplement).

Kazdin, A., Bass, D., Siegel, T., & Thomas, C. (1989). *Journal of Consulting and Psychology, 57,* 522–535.

Kazdin, A., Esveldt-Dawson, K., French, N., & Unis, A. (1987). Problem-solving skills and relationship therapy in the treatment of antisocial child behavior. *Journal of Consulting and Clinical Psychology, 55,* 76–55.

Kazdin, A., & Wilson, G. (1980). *Evaluation of behavioral therapy,* Lincoln: University of Nebraska Press.

Kendall, P., Reber, M., McLeer, S., Epps, J., & Ronan, K. (1990). *Cognitive Therapy and Research, 14,* 279–297.

Kernberg, O. (1986). Identification and its vicissitudes as observed in psychosis. *International Journal of Psycho-Analysis, 67,* 147–159.

Kiesler, C. (1982). Mental hospitals and alternative case. *American Psychologist, 37,* 349–360.

Kiesler, C., & Morton, T. (1988). Psychology and public policy in the "health care revolution." *American Psychologist, 43,* 993–1003.

Kiesler, C., & Sibulkin, A. (1987). *Mental hospitalization: Myths and facts about a national crisis.* Newbury Park, CA: Sage.

King, G., Armitage, S., & Tilton, J. (1960). A therapeutic approach to schizophrenics of extreme pathology: An operant-interpersonal method. *Journal of Abnormal Social Psychology, 61,* 276–286 .

Kirkley, B., Schneider, J., Agras, S., & Bachman, J. (1985). Comparison of two group treatments for bulimia. *Journal of Consulting and Clinical Psychology, 53,* 43–48.

Klein, N., Alexander, J., & Parsons, B. (1977). Impact of family/systems intervention on recidivism and sibling delinquency. *Journal of Consulting and Clinical Psychology, 45,* 469–474.

Klerman, G., DiMascio, A., Weissman, M., Prusoff, B., & Paykel, E. (1974). Treatment of depression by drugs and psychotherapy. *American Journal of Psychiatry, 131,* 186–191.

Klosko, J., Barlow, D., Tassinari, R., & Cerny, J. (1990). A comparison of alprazolam and behavior therapy in the treatment of panic disorder. *Journal of Consulting and Clinical Psychology, 58,* 77–84.

Kohn, E., Ondasik, P., & Repko, D. (1990). Self-insured employers, ERISA, ASO and managed care. In D. Hastings, W. Krasner, J. Michaels, & N. Rosenberg

(Eds.) *The insider's guide to managed care: A legal and operational roadmap.* Washington, DC: National Health Lawyers Association.

Langsley, D., Flomenhaft, K., & Machotka, P. (1969). Follow-up evaluation of family crisis therapy. *American Journal of Orthopsychiatry, 39,* 753–759.

LaPointe, K., & Rimm, D. (1980). Cognitive, assertive, and insight-oriented group therapies in the treatment of reactive depression in women. *Psychotherapy: Theory, Research and Practice, 17,* 312–321.

Lassers, E. (1986). A psychotic recovers: From symbiosis to adulthood. *Journal of Psychoanalysis, 46,* 350–359.

Leff, J., Kuipers, L., Berkowitz, R., & Sturgeon, D. (1982). A controlled study of social intervention in the families of schizophrenic patients. *British Journal of Psychiatry, 141,* 121–134.

Leitenberg, H. (1993). Bulimia nervosa. In T. Giles (Ed.), *Handbook of effective psychotherapy.* New York: Plenum.

Lerner, M., & Clum, G. (1990). Treatment of suicide ideators: A problem-solving approach. *Behavior Therapy , 21,* 403–411.

Levenson, A., Lord, C., Sermas, C., Thornby, J., Sullender, W., & Comstock, B. (1977). Acute schizophrenia: An efficacious outpatient treatment approach as an alternative to full-time hospitalization. *Diseases of the Nervous System,* 242–245.

Levis, D., & Carrera, R. (1967). Effects of ten hours of implosive therapy in the treatment of outpatients: A preliminary report. *Journal of Abnormal Psychology, 72,* 504–508.

Ley, R. (1987). Panic disorders: A hyperventilation interpretation. In L. Michelson & M. Ascher (Eds.), *Anxiety and stress disorders: Cognitive-behavioral assessment and treatment.* New York: Guilford.

Lieberman, R., & Eckman, T. (1981). Behavior therapy versus insight-oriented therapy for repeated suicide attempters. *Archives of General Psychiatry, 38,* 1126–1130.

Lieberman, R., Mueser, K., and Wallace, C. (1986). Social skills training for schizophrenic individuals at risk for relapse. *American Journal of Psychiatry, 143,* 523–526.

Lieberman, R., & Smith, V. (1972). A multiple baseline design of systematic desensitization in a patient with multiple phobias. *Behavior Therapy, 3,* 597–603.

Littleton v. *Good Samaritan Hospital,* 529 N. E. 2d 449 (Ohio 1988).

Lohr, K., Brook, R., Kamberg, C., Goldberg, G., Leibowitz, A., Keesey, J., Reboussin, D., & Newhouse, J. (1986). *Use of medical care in the Rand Health Insurance experiment.* Santa Monica, CA: Rand Corporation.

Longabaugh, R., McCrady, B., Fink, E., Stout, R., McAuley, T., Doyle, C., & McNeill, D. (1983). Cost-effectiveness of alcoholism treatment in partial vs. Inpatient settings: Six-month outcomes. *Journal of Studies of Alcohol, 44,* 1049–1071.

Luborsky, L. (1984). *Principles of psychoanalytic psychotherapy: A manual for supportive-expressive (SE) treatment.* New York: Basic.

Luborsky, L., Singer, B., & Luborsky, L. (1975). Comparative studies of psychotherapies. *Archives of General Psychiatry, 32*, 995–1008.

Ludwigson, K., & Enright, M. (1988). The health care revolution: Implications for psychology and hospital practice. *Psychotherapy, 25*, 424–428.

Luft, H. (1981). *Health maintenance organizations: Dimensions of performance.* New York: Wiley.

Mann, D. (1986). Six months in the treatment of two young chronic schizophrenics. *Psychiatry, 49*, 231–240.

Manning, W., Wells, K., & Benjamin, B. (1987). Use of outpatient mental health services over time in a health maintenance organization. *American Journal of Psychiatry ,144*, 283–287

Markowitz, J., Weissman, M., Ouelette, R., Lish, J., & Klereman, G. (1989). Quality of life in panic disorder. *Archives of General Psychiatry, 46*, 984–992.

Marks, I. (1978). Behavioral psychotherapy of adult neurosis. In S. Garfield & A. Bergin (Eds.), *Handbook of psychotherapy and behavior change.* New York: Wiley.

Marks, I. (1982). Toward an empirical clinical science: Psychotherapy in the 1950s. *Behavior Therapy, 13*, 63–81.

Marks, I., & Gelder, M. (1967). Transvestism and fetishism: Clinical and psychological changes during foradic aversion. *British Journal of Psychiatry, 113*, 711–729.

Mayer, T., & Mayer, G. (1985). HMOs: origins and development. *New England Journal of Medicine, 312*, 590–594.

McLachlan, J., & Stein, R. (1982). Evaluation of a day clinic for alcoholics. *Journal of Studies on Alcohol, 43*, 261–272.

McLean, P., & Hakstian, A. (19–19). Clinical depression: Comparative efficacy of outpatient treatments. *Journal of Consulting and Clinical Psychology, 47*, 818–836.

McLean, P., & Hakstian, A. (1990). Relative endurance of unipolar depression treatment effects: Longitudinal follow-up. *Journal of Consulting and Clinical Psychology, 58*, 482–488.

McLean, P., Ogston, K., & Graverl, L. (1973). A behavioral approach to the treatment of depression. *Journal of Behavior Therapy and Experimental Psychiatry, 4*, 323–330.

Mechanic, D. (1980). *Mental health and social policy* (rev. ed.). Englewood Cliffs, NJ: Prentice-Hall.

Mechanic, D. (1987). Correcting misconception in mental health policy: Strategies of improved care of the seriously mentally ill. *The Milbank Quarterly, 65*, 153–176.

Michelson, L., & Ascher, M. (1987). *Anxiety and stress disorders: Cognitive-behavioral assessment and treatment.* New York: Guilford.

Michelson, L., Mannacino, A., Marchione, K., Stern, M., Figueroa, J., & Beck, S. (1983). A comparative study of behavior social-skills training, interpersonal problem-solving and non-directive control treatments with child psychiatric outpatients. *Behavior Research and Therapy, 21*, 545–556.

Michelson, L., & Marchione, K. (1991). Behavioral, cognitive, and pharmacological treatments of panic disorder with agoraphobia: Critique and synthesis. *Journal of Consulting and Clinical Psychology, 59*, 100–114.

Michelson, L., Marchione, K., & Greenwald, M. (1989). *Cognitive-behavioral treatments of agoraphobia.* Association for the Advancement of Behavior Therapy, Washington, DC.

Milby, J., & Meredith, R. (1980). Obsessive-compulsive disorders. In R. Daitzman (Ed.), *Clinical behavior therapy and behavior modification.* New York: Garland.

Miller, I., Norman, W., Keinter, L., Bishop, B., and Dow, M. (1989). Cognitive-behavioral treatment of depressed inpatients. *Behavior Therapy, 20*, 25–47.

Miller, P., Hersen, M., Eisler, R., & Watts, J. (1974). Contingent reinforcement of lowered blood alcohol levels in an outpatient chronic alcoholic. *Behavior Research and Therapy, 5*, 15–18.

Miller, W. (1982). Treating problem drinkers: What works, *Behavior Therapist, 5*, 15–18.

Miller, W., & Hester, R. (1986). Inpatient alcohol treatment. *American Psychologist, 41*, 794–805.

Mills, L., Agras, W., Barlow, D., & Mills, J. (1973). Compulsive rituals treated by response prevention: An experimental analysis. *Archives of General Psychiatry, 28*, 524–529.

Mines, R. (1990). *Efforts to control health and mental health costs.* Office of the Governor, Symposium of Communities for a Drug-Free Colorado, Denver. CO.

Minuchin, S., Rosman, B., & Baker, L. (1978.). *Psychosomatic families: Anorexia nervosa in context.* Cambridge, MA: Harvard University Press.

Mitchell, J., Pyle, R., Elkert, E., Hatsukami, D., Pomeroy, C., & Zimmerman, R. (1990). A Comparistudy of antidepressants and structured group therapy in the treatment of bulimia nervosa. *Archives of General Psychiatry, 47*, 149–157.

Moreno, A. (1981). The treatment of obsessive compulsive disorders: An outcome study. In W. Minsel & W. Herff (Eds.), *Research on Psychotherapeutic Approaches.* New York: Peter Lang.

Moreno, A. (1983). *Experimental analysis of comparative psychotherapy.* Unpublished manuscript. University Complutense de Madrid.

Morris, N. (1978). A group self-instruction method for the treatment of depressed outpatients. *Dissertation Abstracts International, 38*, 4473–4474.

Mosher, L., Menn, A., & Matthews, S. (1975). Soteria: Evaluation of a home-based treatment for schizophrenia. *American Journal of Ortho-psychiatry, 45*, 455–467.

Mueser, K., & Berenbaum, H. (1990). Psychodynamic treatment of schizophrenia: Is there a future? *Psychological Medicine, 2*, 253–262.

Mumford, E., Schlesinger, H., & Glass, G. (1982). The effects of psychological intervention on recovery from surgery and heart attacks: An analysis of the literature. *American Journal of Public Health, 72*, 141–151.

Mumford, E., Schlesinger, H., Glass, G., Patrick, C., & Cuerdon, T. (1984). A new look at evidence about reduced cost of medical utilization following mental health treatment. *American Journal of Psychiatry, 141*, 1145–1158.

Munich, R. (1987). Conceptual-trends and issues in the psychotherapy of schizophrenia. *American Journal of Psychotherapy, 41*, 23–37.

Nader, R. (1965). *Unsafe at any speed*. New York: Grossman.

Ney, P., Palvesky, A., & Markely, J. (1971). Relative effectiveness of operant conditioning and play therapy in childhood schizophrenia. *Journal of Autism and Childhood Schizophrenia, 1*, 337–349.

Nezu, A. (1986). Efficacy of social problem-solving therapy for unipolar depression: An initial dismantling investigation. *Journal of Consulting and Clinical Psychology, 57*, 408–413.

Orford, J., Oppenheimer, E., & Edwards, G. (1976). Abstinence or control: The outcome for excessive drinkers two years after consultation. *Behavior Research and Therapy, 14*, 409–418.

Parker, S., & Knoll, J. (1990). Partial hospitalization: An update. *American Journal of Psychiatry, 147*, 156–160.

Parsons, B., & Alexander, J. (1973). Short-term family intervention: A therapy outcome study. *Journal of Consulting and Clinical Psychology, 41*, 195–201.

Pasamanick, B., Scarpitti, F., & Dinitz, S. (1967). *Schizophrenics and the community*. New York: Appleton-Century-Crofts.

Patterson, G. (1982). *Coercing family process*. Eugene, OR: Castalia.

Patterson, G., Chamberlain, N., & Dishion, N. (1993). Conduct and oppositional disorders: A review of comparative outcome. In T. Giles (Ed.), *Handbook of effective psychotherapy*. New York: Plenum.

Patterson, G., Chamberlain, P., & Reid, J. (1992). Comparative efficacy of parent training for conduct-disordered youth. *Behavior Therapy, 13*, 638–650.

Patterson, G., & Forgatch, M. (1987). *Living together, Part 1: The basics*. Eugene, OR: Castalia.

Paul, G. (1966). *Insight vs. desensitization in psychotherapy*. Stanford, CA: Stanford University Press.

Paul, G. (1967). Insight vs. desensitization in psychotherapy two years after termination. *Journal of Consulting and Clinical Psychology, 31*, 333–348.

Paul, G. (1969). Outcome of systematic desensitization II. In C. M. Franks (Ed.) *Behavior therapy appraisal and status*. New York: McGraw-Hill.

Paul, G., & Lentz, R. (1977). *Psychological treatment of chronic mental patients: Milieu versus social-learning programs*. Cambridge, MA: Harvard University Press.

Pauly, M. (1968). The economics of moral hazard: Comment. *American Economic Review, 21*, 531–537.

Pekarik, G. (1983). Follow-up adjustment of outpatient dropouts. *American Journal of Orthopsychiatry, 53*, 501–511.

Pekarik, G. (1986). The use of treatment termination status and duration patterns as an indication of treatment effectiveness. *Evaluation and Program Planning, 19*, 25–30.

Pekarik, G. (1989). *Consumer preference: Psychotherapy dropout and treatment*. Minneapolis: MCC, Inc.

Pekarik, G. (1993). Brief therapy and consumer preference: A review. In T. Giles (Ed.), *Handbook of effective psychotherapy*. New York: Plenum.

Polak, P., & Kirby, M. (1976). A model to replace psychiatric hospitals. *Journal of Nervous and Mental Disorders, 162,* 13–22.

Pope, H., Hudson, J., Jonas, J., & Yurgelin-Todd, D. (1985). Antidepressant treatment of bulimia: A two-year follow-up study. *Journal of Clinical Psychopharmacology, 5,* 320–327.

Rachman, S., & Hodgson, R. (1980). *Obsessions and compulsions.* Englewood Cliffs: NJ: Prentice Hall.

Rachman, S., & Wilson, G. (1980). *The effects of Psychological therapy.* London: Pergamon.

Rimland, B. (1977). *Comparative effects of treatment on child's behavior (drugs, therapies, schooling, and several non-treatment events).* Institute for Child Behavior Research, publication 34.

Robinson, J. (1991). *Perspectives on managed care.* Annual Residents' Seminar, Colorado Health Sciences Center, Denver, CO.

Robinson, C., & Luft, H. (1987). Competition and the cost of hospital care, 1972–1982. *Journal of the American Medical Association, 257,* 3241–3245.

Roemer, R. (1985). I. S. Falk, the committee on costs of medical care, and the drive for national health insurance. *American Journal of Public Health, 75,* 841–848.

Rosen, J. (1990). *Outcome predictors in bulimia nervosa.* San Francisco: Association for the Advancement of Behavior Therapy.

Rosen, J., & Leitenberg, H. (1982). Bulimia nervosa: Treatment with exposure and response prevention. *Behavior Therapy, 13,* 117–124.

Rosenhan, D. (1975). On being sane in an insane place. *Science, 179,* 250–258.

Rundle, R. (1987). Medical debate: Doctors who oppose the spread of HMOs are losing their fight. *Wall Street Journal,* October 6.

Salter, A. (1963). *The case against psychoanalysis.* New York: Harper and Row.

Samuelson, P., & Nordhaus, W. (1989.) *Economics* (13th ed.). New York: McGraw-Hill.

Schuster V. Altenberg, 424 N. W. 2d 159 (Wis. 1988).

Schwartz, J., & Bellack, A. (1975). A comparison of a token economy with standard inpatient treatment. *Journal of Consulting and Clinical Psychology, 43,* 107–108.

Searles, J. (1985). A methodological critique of psychotherapy outcome meta-analysis. *Behavior Research and Therapy, 23,* 458–463.

Sharfstein, S. (1978). Third-party payers: To pay or not to pay. *American Journal of Psychiatry, 135,* 1185–1188.

Sharfstein, S., & Taube, C. (1982). Reduction in insurance for mental disorders: Adverse selection, moral hazard, and consumer demand. *American Journal of Psychiatry, 139,* 1425–1430.

Shaw, R., (1977). Comparison of cognitive therapy and behavior therapy in the treatment of depression. *Journal of Consulting and Clinical Psychology, 45,* 543–551.

Sherry, P., Mines, R., & Giles, T. (manuscript in preparation). Ethical issues in managed mental health care.

Short, T., & Goldfarb, M. (1987). Redistribution of revenues under a prototypical prospective payment system: Characteristics of winners and loser. *Journal of Policy Analysis and Management, 6*, 385–401.

Siu, A., Leibowitz, A., Brook, R., Goldman, N., Lurie, N., & Newhouse, J. (1988). Use of the hospital in a randomized trial of prepaid care. *Journal of the American Medical Association, 259*, 1343–1346.

Sloan, D., & Chmel, M. (1991). *The quality revolution and health care: A primer for purchasers and providers*. New York: American Society for Quality Control.

Sloane, R., Staples, F., Cristol, A., Yorkston, N., & Whipple, K. (1975). *Psychotherapy vs. behavior therapy*. Cambridge, MA: Harvard University Press.

Smart, R., Finley, J., & Funston, R. (1977). The effectiveness of post-detoxification admissions, drunkenness and criminality. *Drug and Alcohol Dependence, 2*, 149–155.

Smith, D., & Mahoney, J. (1990). *McDonnell Douglas Corporation employee assistance program financial offset study: 1985–1989*. Westport, CT: Alexander and Alexander Consulting Group.

Smith, M., & Glass, G. (1977.). Meta–analysis of psychotherapy outcome studies. *American Psychologist, 132*, 752–760.

Snyder, D., Wills, R., & Grady-Fletcher, A. (1991). Long-term effectiveness of behavioral versus insight-oriented marital therapy: A 4-year follow-up study. *Journal of Consulting and Clinical Psychology, 59*, 138–141.

Sokol, L., Beck, A., Greenberg, R., Berchick, R., & Wright, E. (1989a). *A controlled treatment trial of cognitive therapy for panic disorder*. World Congress of Cognitive Therapy, Oxford, England.

Sokol, L., Beck, A., Greenberg, R., Berchick, R., & Wright, E. (1989b). Cognitive therapy of panic disorder: A nonpharmacological alternative. *Journal of Nervous and Mental Diseases, 177*, 711–716.

Stalcup, A. (1989). *Neurotransmission during withdrawal from crack cocaine*. Invited paper, MCC Cos., Inc. Minneapolis, MN.

Stanton, A., Gunderson, J., Knapp, P., Frank, A., Vannicelli, B., Schnitzer, D., & Rosenthal, R. (1984). Effects of psychotherapy in schizophrenia: I. Design and implementation of a controlled study. *Schizophrenia Bulletin, 10*, 520–653.

Stein, L., Test, M., & Marx, A. (1975). Alternative to the hospital: A controlled study. *American Journal of Psychiatry, 132*, 517–521.

Steketee, G. (1993). Obsessive-compulsive disorder. In T. Giles (Ed.), *Handbook of effective psychotherapy*. New York: Plenum.

Stepakoff, v. Kantar, 473 N. E. 2d 1131 (Mass., 1985).

Steuer, J., Mintz, J., Hammen, C., Hill, M., Jarvik, L., McCarley, T., Motvike, P., & Rosen, R. (1984). Cognitive behavioral and psychodynamic group psychotherapy in treatment of geriatric depression. *Journal of Consulting and Clinical Psychology, 52*, 180–189.

Stiles, W., Shapiro, D., & Elliott, R. (1986). Are all psychotherapies equivalent? *American Psychologist, 41*, 165–180.

Stinson, D., Smith, W., Amidjaya, I., & Kaplan, J. (1979). Systems of care and treatment outcomes for alcoholic patients. *Archives of General Psychiatry, 36,* 535–539.

Strean, H. (1988). *Behind the couch.* New York: Wiley.

Strupp, H., & Binder, J. (1984). *Psychotherapy in a new guide to time-limited dynamic psychotherapy.* New York: Basic.

Strupp, H., & Hadley, S. (1979). Specific versus non-specific factors in psychotherapy: A controlled study of outcome. *Archives of General Psychiatry, 36,* 1125–1136.

Stuart, R. (1977). *Trick or treatment.* Champaign, IL: Research Press.

Sweet, A., Giles, T., & Young, R. (1987). Three theoretical perspectives on anxiety: A comparison of theory and outcome. In L. Michelson and M. Ascher (Eds.), *Anxiety and stress disorders: Cognitive-behavioral assessment and treatment.* New York: Guilford.

Szapocznik, J., Murray, E., Scopetta, M., Hervis, O., Rio, A., Cohen, R., & Rivas-Vasquez, J., & Posada, V. (1989). Structural family versus psychodynamic child therapy for problematic Hispanic boys. *Journal of Consulting and Clinical Psychology, 57,* 571–578.

Telch, M., Agras, W., Taylor, C., Roth, W., & Gallen, C. (1985). Combined pharmacological and behavioral treatment for agoraphobia. *Behavior Research and Therapy, 23,* 325–335.

Townsend, R., House, J., & Addario, D. (.1975). A comparison of biofeedback-mediated relaxation and group therapy in the treatment of chronic anxiety. *American journal of psychology, 132,* 598–601.

TPF&C (1990). *Emphasis.* New York: Tillinghast.

Turner, R., & Ascher, M. (1979). A within-subject analysis of stimulus control therapy with severe sleep-onset insomnia. *Behavior Research and Therapy, 17,* 107–112.

VandenBos, G. (1983). Health financing, service utilization, and national policy: A conversation with Stan Jones. *American Psychologist, 38,* 948–955.

Watzlawick, P., Weakland, J., & Fish, R. (1974) *Change: Principles of problem formation and Problem resolution.* New York: Norton.

Weissman, M., & Merikangas, K. (1986). The epidemiology of anxiety and panic disorder: An update. *Journal of Clinical Psychiatry, 47,* 11–17.

Weisz, J., Weiss, B., Alicke, M., & Klotz, M. (1987). Effectiveness of psychotherapy with children and adolescents: A meta-analysis for clinicians. *Journal of Consulting and Clinical Psychology, 55,* 542–549.

Wilson, A., White, J., & Lange, D. (1978). Outcome evaluation of a hospital-based alcoholism treatment programme. *British Journal of Addiction, 73,* 39–45.

Wilson, G., & O'Leary, K. (1980). *Principles of behavior therapy.* Englewood Cliffs, NJ: Prentice Hall.

Wilson, G., & Rachman, S. (1983). Meta-analysis and the evaluation of psychotherapy outcome: Limitations and liabilities. *Journal of Consulting and Clinical Psychology, 51,* 54–64.

Wolpe, J. (1958). *Psychotherapy by reciprocal inhibition.* Stanford, CA: Stanford University Press.

Wolpe, J. (1977). Inadequate behavior analysis: The Achilles heel of outcome research in behavior therapy. *Journal of Behavior Therapy and Experimental Psychiatry, 8,* 1–3.

Wolpe, J. (1986). The positive diagnosis of neurotic depression as on etiological category. *Comprehensive Psychiatry, 27,* 449–460.

Wolpe, J. (1990). *The practice of behavior therapy* (4th ed.). Oxford: Pergamon Press.

Wolpe, J., Giles, T., & Phillis, R. (1992). *Your mind and your money: The new Psychotherapies.* New York: Avery.

Zilbergeld, B. (1983). *The shrinking of America.* New York: Little-Brown.

Zook, C., Moore, F., & Zeckhauser, R. (1981). "Catastrophic" health insurance—A misguided prescription? *The Public Interest, 62* 66–81.

Author Index

Subject Index

Psychology Practitioner
Guidebooks

Stress Inoculation Training
Donald Meichenbaum
ISBN: 0–205–14418–7

**Management of Chronic Headaches:
A Psychological Approach**
Edward B. Blanchard & Fran Andrasik
ISBN: 0–205–14284–2

Clinical Utilization of Microcomputer Technology
Raymond G. Romanczyk
ISBN: 0–205–14468–3

**Marital Therapy: A Behavioral-
Communications Approach**
Philip H. Bornstein & Marcy T. Bornstein
ISBN: 0–205–14289–3

Psychological Consultation in the Courtroom
Michael T. Nietzel & Ronald C. Dillehay
ISBN: 0–205–14426–8

**Group Cognitive Therapy: A Treatment Approach for
Depressed Older Adults**
Elizabeth E. Yost, Larry E. Beutler, M. Anne Corbishley
& James R. Allender
ISBN: 0–205–14516–7

Dream Analysis in Psychotherapy
Lillie Weiss
ISBN: 0–205–14499–3

**Understanding and Treating Attention
Deficient Disorder**
Edward A. Kirby & Liam K. Grimley
ISBN: 0–205–14391–1

Language and Speech Disorders in Children
Jon Eisenson
ISBN: 0–205–14315–6

Adolescent Anger Control: Cognitive-Behavioral Techniques
Eva L. Feindler & Randolph B. Ecton
ISBN: 0–205–14324–5

Pediatric Psychology: Psychological Interventions and Strategies for Pediatric Problems
Michael C. Roberts
ISBN: 0–205–14465–9

Treating Childhood and Adolescent Obesity
Daniel S. Kirschenbaum, William G. Johnson & Peter M. Stalonas, Jr.
ISBN: 0–205–14393–8

Eating Disorders: Management of Obesity, Bulimia and Anorexia Nervosa
W. Stewart Agras
ISBN: 0–205–14262–1

Treatment of Depression: An Interpersonal Systems Approach
Ian H. Gotlib & Catherine A. Colby
ISBN: 0–205–14357–1

Psychology as a Profession: Foundations of Practice
Walter B. Pryzwansky & Robert N. Wendt
ISBN: 0–205–14459–4

Multimethod Assessment of Chronic Pain
Paul Karoly & Mark P. Jensen
ISBN: 0–205–14385–7

Hypnotherapy: A Modern Approach
William L. Golden, E. Thomas Dowd & Fred Friedberg
ISBN: 0–205–14334–2

Behavioral Treatment for Persistent Insomnia
Patricia Lacks
ISBN: 0–205–14399–7

The Physically and Sexually Abused Child:
Evaluation and Treatment
C. Eugene Walker, Barbara L. Bonner & Keith L. Kaufman
ISBN: 0–205–14493–4

Social Skills Training Treatment for Depression
Robert E. Becker, Richard G. Heimberg & Alan S. Bellack
ISBN: 0–205–14273–7

Teaching Child Management Skills
Richard F. Dangel & Richard A. Polster
ISBN: 0–205–14308–3

Rational-Emotive Therapy with Alcoholics and
Substance Abusers
Albert Ellis, John F. McInerney, Raymond DiGiuseppe &
Raymond J. Yeager
ISBN: 0–205–14320–2

Non-Drug Treatments for Essential Hypertension
Edward B. Blanchard, John E. Martin
& Patricia M. Dubbert
ISBN: 0–205–14286–9

Treating Obsessive-Compulsive Disorder
Samuel M. Turner & Deborah C. Beidel
ISBN: 0–205–14488–8

Self-Esteem Enhancement with Children
and Adolescents
Alice W. Pope, Susan M. McHale &
W. Edward Craighead
ISBN: 0–205–14455–1

Preventing Substance Abuse Among
Children and Adolescents
Jean E. Rhodes & Leonard A. Jason
ISBN: 0–205–14463–2

Clinical Practice in Adoption
Robin C. Winkler, Dirck W. Brown,
Margaret van Keppel & Amy Blanchard
ISBN: 0–205–14512–4

Behavioral Relaxation Training and Assessment
Roger Poppen
ISBN: 0–205–14457–8

Adult Obesity Therapy
Michael D. LeBow
ISBN: 0–205–14404–7

Social Skills Training for Psychiatric Patients
Robert Paul Liberman, William J. DeRisi & Kim T. Mueser
ISBN: 0–205–14406–3

Treating Depression in Children and Adolescents
Johnny L. Matson
ISBN: 0–205–14414–4

The Practice of Brief Psychotherapy
Sol L. Garfield
ISBN: 0–205–14329–6

Reducing Delinquency:
Intervention in the Community
Arnold P. Goldstein, Barry Glick, Mary Jane Irwin, Claudia
Pask-McCartney & Ibrahim Rubama
ISBN: 0–205–14338–5

Rational-Emotive Couples Therapy
Albert Ellis, Joyce L. Sichel, Raymond J. Yeager,
Dominic J. DiMattia, & Raymond DiGiuseppe
ISBN: 0–205–14317–2 Paper   0–205–14433–0 Cloth

Cognitive-Behavioral Interventions with Young Offenders
Clive R. Hollin
ISBN: 0–205–14368–7 Paper   0–205–14369–5 Cloth

Gestalt Therapy: Practice and Theory, Second Edition
Margaret P. Korb, Jeffrey Gorrell & Vernon Van De Riet
ISBN: 0–205–14395–4 Paper   0–205–14396–2 Cloth

Assessment of Eating Disorders: Obesity, Anorexia
and Bulimia Nervosa
Donald A. Williamson
ISBN: 0–205–14507–8 Paper   0–205–14508–6 Cloth

Body Image Disturbance: Assessment and Treatment
J. Kevin Thompson
ISBN: 0–205–14482–9 Paper   0–205–14483–7 Cloth

Suicide Risk: Assessment and Response Guidelines
William J. Fremouw, Maria de Perczel & Thomas E. Ellis
ISBN: 0–205–14327–X Paper   0–205–14328–8 Cloth

**Treating Conduct and Oppositional Defiant
Disorders in Children**
Arthur M. Horne & Thomas V. Sayger
ISBN: 0–205–14371–7 Paper   0–205–14372–5 Cloth

Counseling the Bereaved
Richard A. Dershimer
ISBN: 0–205–14310–5 Paper   0–205–14311–3 Cloth

Behavioral Medicine: Concepts and Procedures
Eldon Tunks & Anthony Bellissimo
ISBN: 0–205–14484–5 Paper   0–205–14485–3 Cloth

Drug Therapy for Behavior Disorders: An Introduction
Alan Poling, Kenneth D. Gadow & James Cleary
ISBN: 0–205–14453–5 Paper   0–205–14454–3 Cloth

**The Personality Disorders:
A Psychological Approach to Clinical Management**
Ira Daniel Turkat
ISBN: 0–205–14486–1 Paper   0–205–14487–X Cloth

**Treatment of Rape Victims:
Facilitating Psychosocial Adjustment**
Karen S. Calhoun & Beverly M. Atkeson
ISBN: 0–205–14296–6 Paper   0–205–14297–4 Cloth

**Psychotherapy and Counseling with Minorities:
A Cognitive Approach to Individual and Cultural Differences**
Manuel Ramirez III
ISBN: 0–205–14461–6

Coping with Ethical Dilemmas in Psychotherapy
Martin Lakin
ISBN: 0–205–14401–2 Paper   0–205–14402–0 Cloth

Anxiety Disorders: A Rational-Emotive Perspective
Ricks Warren & George D. Zgourides
ISBN: 0–205–14497–7 Paper   0–205–14498–5 Cloth

Preventing Relapse in the Addictions:
A Biopsychosocial Approach
Emil J. Chiauzzi
ISBN: 0–205–14303–2 Paper   0–205–14304–0 Cloth

Behavioral Family Intervention
Matthew R. Sanders & Mark R. Dadds
ISBN: 0–205–14599–X Paper   0–205–14600–7 Cloth

Anxiety Disorders in Youth:
Cognitive-Behavioral Interventions
Philip C. Kendall
ISBN: 0–205–14589–2 Paper   0–205–14590–6 Cloth

Psychological Treatment of Cancer Patients:
A Cognitive-Behavioral Approach
William L. Golden, Wayne D. Gersh & David M. Robbins
ISBN: 0–205–14551–5 Paper   0–205–14552–3 Cloth

School Consultation: Practice and Training,
Second Edition
Jane Close Conoley & Collie W. Conoley
ISBN: 0–205–14561–2 Paper   0–205–14564–7 Cloth

Posttraumatic Stress Disorder: A Behavioral Approach
to Assessment and Treatment
Philip A. Saigh
ISBN: 0–205–14553–1 Paper   0–205–14554–X Cloth

Cognitive Therapy of Borderline Personality Disorder
Mary Anne Layden, Cory F. Newman, Arthur Freeman
& Susan B. Byers
ISBN: 0–205–14808–5 Paper   0–205–14807–7 Cloth

Social Skills for Mental Health:
A Structured Learning Approach
Robert P. Sprafkin, N. Jane Gershaw & Arnold P. Goldstein
ISBN: 0–205–14842–5 Paper   0–205–14841–7 Cloth

Managed Mental Health Care: A Guide for Practitioners, Employers, and Hospital Administrators
Thomas R. Giles
ISBN: 0–205–14839–5 Paper   0–205–14838–7 Cloth